ALTERNATIVE CREATIONIST THEORIES AND HISTORY DRAWN FROM THE BIBLE

Curtis Hatfield

XULON PRESS

ALTERNATIVE CREATIONIST THEORIES AND HISTORY DRAWN FROM THE BIBLE

But, beloved, be not ignorant of this one thing, that one day is with the Lord as a thousand years, and a thousand years as one day.

II Peter 3:8

That means that the creation (organigation from eternally existing matter) of this earth took seven thousand years which includes a day of rest. This provided sufficient time for things to happen that are found in earths geologic records.

Foreword

The Scripture is our Creator, organizer or manufacturer's operation and repair manual for best use of our mortal bodies.

Each theory is just that, a theory explaining a situation or condition that may or may not be true. All theories provide a framework to invite study and testing for elements of truth.

Our Omniscient (all knowing of eternal Telestial, Terrestrial and Celestial laws) Creator, ten times in the first chapter of Genesis, makes it clear that each true species will be limited to reproducing "after its own kind". Genesis 1:1–25

Devotees of the evolutionary theory of creation have made of it their religious faith, and they are not open to other points of view, regardless of the evidence.

There may be a few with open minds, and to these and those without any particular position, this book is addressed. There are many events, witnessed as history in the Scriptures, which these theoretical "scientists" have avoided. They refuse to discuss them as real meaningful events, because they do not want to acknowledge a creator who will expect them to live by principles vs. a law-unto-self concept and will require their Final Judgment.

They purposefully conjure up vast millennia of dating schemes based on the sequence of strata layers. (Time gives feasibility to weak theories.) See II Peter 3:8.

The prophet, witnesses at the direction of the Creator (our Lord and Savior) do not discuss time much beyond 13,000 years B.C. It appears that when our Creator (possibly with our help) organized this earth, it was done as one would roll up a snowman. To add the "plenty and to spare" of basic natural resources, he probably moved it to where the needed elements were floating in space. Then added some iron, copper, silver, gold, etc., as desired.

Visualize a horizon filled with an ancient city with all its flatroofed structures, etc. Now visualize it catching on fire, a tornado, an earthquake, a lava covering, etc., etc., until there is nothing left except rubble. Now ask yourself the honest question.

Which account of the history of that scene is more valid? A: The living witness escaped to a cave where God inspired them to make a first hand record of what they saw? Or, B: Highly educated theory "scientists", looking at and examining the rubble and devising a somewhat logical dream solution? When comparing the two options, it's time to "get real".

Your author has depended on referencing and making available to the reader pertinent scriptures. However, since others have provided first-rate in-depth research that supports my positions, it is best to encourage the reader to go through interlibrary loan or other process to review the factual research cited.

Immanuel Velikovsky is best, and his best book in support of cataclysmic changes is *Earth in Upheaval*. However, all of his books support biblical events, although he never mentions the Bible. He holds and earned Ph.D. in seven different disciplines, making him one of the best-educated men ever on earth. He was friend and co-researcher with Albert Einstein at Princeton. On the day of his death, Einstein, with a Velikovsky book on his desk, is reported by *Readers Digest as* saying, "We've got to afford Velikovsky's works greater credence."

A second witness author researcher to bring to readers' attention is Steven A. Austin, and his book, *Catastrophes in Earth History*. A third, recently published, book is by eminent lawyer, Jerome Horowitz, who answers the question, *Evolution: Is it Science or Faith?*

Of recent interest is the subject of asteroid strikes on earth and the changes to the surface of the earth related to the size and speed of the asteroid. See Chapter XVIII.

Preface

This book is designed to assist parents in their proper desire that local schools be permitted to offer their children a creationist theory for the origin of life. Creationism should be taught on an equal and uncensored basis with the repetitious but very questionable theory of biological evolution.

Evolution was first taught by the ancient Greeks and has remained an unproven theory for over 2,500 years. It was resurrected by Charles Darwin and his disciples. We must remember that a theory is just a theory if it cannot be proven as fact by visual or demonstrable proof. Why should public servants, school boards or teachers or anyone else object to alternative teachings and theories as a basis for opening the minds of students? Is there a danger in giving each child or youth the opportunity to make their own objective choice from an alternative theory, based on faith in an omniscient God versus an imaginary improvement of life forms based on blind chance.

The intent of the author is to support and assist parents in obtaining a creationist education on an equal basis with the theory of evolution.

Eden is depicted at 4127 B.C. per Genesis 1, 2 and other scriptures. Approximate dating from 964 B.C. start of Solomon Reign is scripturally supported within a 30-year + or - deviation.

Probably when the city of Enoch was taken from the earth, the earth rotated counter clock wise 90 to 103 degrees far new north pole per tropical flora and fauna found in Alaska and Siberia*

The earth was organized from eternal matter over a 7000- year span. See II Peter 3:8. Many post-Eden cataclysms have changed its water and land surface in the 2500 years sink the flood and the Ice age following it

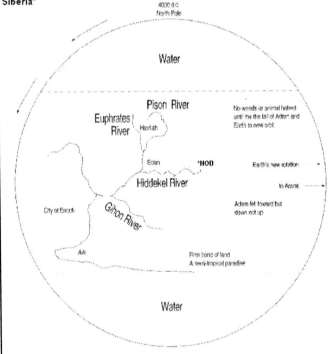

4000 B.C
North Pole

Water

Pison River

Euphrates River

Haviah

No weeds or animal hatred until the the fall of Adam and Earth to new orbit

Eden

*NOD

Earth's new rotation

Hiddekel River

to Ararat

City of Enoch

Gihon River

Adam fell forward but down not up

Ark

Firm band of land
A semi-tropical paradise

Water

*See Joshua 10:13
Genesis 7:11-24
     10:21-25, 32
Also: Earth in Upheaval by Emmanuel Velikovsky, friend of Albert Einstein at Princeton University, USA

Pre-flood, Enoch and his city were taken from Earth. Post-flood, the Ark rested on Ararat in the eastern hemisphere.

The Earth in the Dispensation of Adam

Contents

Genesis Creationist Theory and Assumption I

HOW EARTH WAS CREATED/ORGANIZED

Book of Genesis
"In the beginning God created the heaven and the earth." This first statement, which gives no clue as to the method used, invites a multitude of theories for explanation. However, since all truths are in harmony, it is obvious that true science and true religious understanding will eventually lead to the same conclusions. It is assumed that an intelligent God caused the earth to be rolled through the differing elements of eternally existing matter floating in space. Layer upon layer of strata was probably formed as one would use snow to form a snowman.

We assume the recent finding of science that matter is indestructible is true. Its form may be changed to vapor for instance, but all of it still exists.

Genesis Creationist Theory and Assumption II

HOW ALL PLANT AND ANIMAL LIFE CAME TO EARTH

Book of Genesis

The raw material floating in outer space contains all the natural resources required to support life, as we know it on this planet. The amounts and placement of those elements required super intelligent management. For instance, after the earth was formed of rock and water and put in rotation to provide night and day, seasons, etc., how was a breathable atmosphere, with its fine balanced envelope of oxygen and carbon dioxide, organized and how did life begin on earth? The order of creation indicates that after water and sunlight were provided, plant life came next.

Where did it come from? If each separate species of plant and animal life conformed to God's law, each would reproduce "after its own kind" (suggest the reader underline in red the number of times a phrase similar to that is repeated in just the first chapter of Genesis). This leaves but one conclusion, that all forms of life on this earth were transplanted from previously functioning older earths within the universe. It is recognized that this does not completely answer theories of the evolution of species. However, it does remove it from our egocentric philosophy that all life developed on this earth. Science has recently (1999) proved the existence of other (some probably inhabited) earths in other solar systems.

Plant life was first, according to all scriptural accounts. Animal life, which is dependent on oxygen, followed 1,000 years or a millennium, after plants. Plants using naturally occurring carbon dioxide began growing and multiplying within their various transplanted species. They began expelling oxygen and one wonders how enough oxygen accumulated to make it possible for all forms of animal life to live and breathe in a perfectly balanced atmosphere or stage of development. How (and in what form) lower animal flesh forms were transported to earth is not suggested by the scripture. Seeds were no doubt transported from earth to earth, just as a farmer plants seeds or transplants from field to field. The millennial days required for this are clearly explained in II Peter 3:8 and other scripture. But extinct life forms remain available on other planets in space.

God has stated that all forms of life "fill the measure of their creation" before death and extinction. Extinction is a natural law not accepted and understood by our legislative bodies and others. When the need for a species or its habitat is gone, it becomes extinct on a given earth. This could be termed the merciful law of extinction. We should be grateful not to have to face dinosaurs on our morning walk.

The second basic theory is that dinosaurs were sent as an early large animal in order to provide enough oxygen. Their breathing out of massive amounts of carbon dioxide caused the vast primordial forests to flourish, which in turn produced large amounts of oxygen resulting in the oxygen-carbon dioxide balance enjoyed by all forms of life, from Adam to the present. It is probable that minute forms of plant and animal life were transplanted in an orderly fashion until there was food for introduction of larger forms.

Genesis Creationist Theory and Assumption III

HOW MANKIND CAME TO EARTH

Book of Genesis

This flora and fauna developed rapidly. At first the earth (terra firma) stood above the massive oceans at each of the poles. The land mass was a tropical paradise that circumscribed the whole central portion or band around the earth.

How Adam's mortal body was developed is veiled in a myth that serves as the boundary to the understanding given to man versus that enjoyed by God. We would do very well if we could master the truths of this earth and learn the knowledge of higher realms, after our entrance to those realms. We can observe that our flesh is created and enjoys health and growth from elements (flora and fauna) derived originally from the dust of the earth. The natural birth of our pre-mortal spirit bodies is made understandable to us through the life cycle of various forms of life placed on earth by the Lord.

One well-known example is the life cycle of the butterfly, which could be called the revelator species as it tells man so much about his own life. It begins life in a cocoon, which could be likened to man's pre-mortal spirit birth. At a given point, the living element of the cocoon animates as a caterpillar body and it lives a mobile existence as such. This could be likened to our birth where our resurrected God parent arranged for our earthly parents to prepare a sacred mortal tabernacle into which our spirits enter at birth. Verification is available by a multitude of witnesses who agree with some Jewish teachers who tell us that the spirit world is but 50 cubits (75 to 100 feet) above the earth's surface. See John 1:1–14, 8:58, 17:5, I Peter 1:20, Ecclesiastes 12:7, Hebrews 12:9, Job 12:10, Isaiah 57:16, Revelation 12:7–11.

No one questions the pre-mortality of Jesus Christ, he being the

Old Testament Jehovah God, functioning in a pre-mortal spirit body. Read St. John 9:1–2 and it is plain that all mankind had a pre-mortal spirit body existence.

From these assurances we can draw some basic assumptions about Jehovah, Elohim or God the Father, Adam and ourselves.

First, only resurrected Gods with celestial bodies are capable of giving birth to spirit-bodied children.

These spirits are material in nature but their elements are so fine and pure that they are not visible to the naturally unprepared mortal eye. If one places a hand on a desk, they leave a material substance that cannot be seen by the non-microscopically assisted mortal eye. Only through a microscope can our eyes observe the bacteria left on the desk. In a like manner, only a person prepared by the Lord as a "Seer" is capable of seeing the many spirit bodies which are associated to or assigned to this earth.

Second, these spirit bodies, as well as the Terrestrial type bodies of Adam and Eve before their fall, have no power to reproduce.

Third, mortal bodies contain mortal blood, which has more iron and other elements than the very similar chlorophyll fluid, which acts as blood for plant life. The two fluids, blood in plasma and chlorophyll, are very similar except that blood has iron in it. The purposeful mystery, with which Jehovah (the God in the Spirit Body) surrounded the creation of man, may hint that Eve was cloned.

Fourth, all must pass through death (a separation of body and spirit) to resurrect or rejoin body to spirit. In resurrected form each will have an immortal body like that unto the light or glory of the Telestial* (stars) Terrestrial (moon), or Celestial (sun). Only celestial spiritualized bodies gain power to reproduce spirit children eternally. Obtaining a celestial body is dependent on the level of the laws one is willing to put oneself in harmony with during one's earthly test. See I Corinthians 15:38–58. Only the valiant in living God's Celestial Laws become the full-fledged Gods referred to in St. John 10:34–35, Psalms 82:6 and Romans 8:16, 10:13–21.

The name of the Glory signified by stars "Telestial" was lost from N.T. but has been used for 170 years and is clearly understood by 12 million people today (dictionary deficiency).

Shortly after their arrival on earth, Adam and Eve literally ate a fruit that changed the fluid in their veins to red mortal blood. The original sin was not a sex sin because God had married or given Eve to Adam. Mortality made them capable of reproduction, but subject to aging and death. Virtuous chastity is not forfeited when the marriage is approved by the laws of God and/or men. Either the transplantation of Adam's spirit to be placed within his body, on this earth, or his mortality began, after taking the fruit, about 4127 B.C.

Genesis Creationist Theory and Assumption IV

ORGANIC EVOLUTION REFUTED, MAN'S DESTINY BY OBEDIENCE TO GOD

Book of Genesis
Although man is lumped together with all other animals in biology as a single flesh and fauna division, I Corinthians 15:39–40 makes it clear that there are four completely separate species of flesh, i.e. man, beast, fish and fowl and each reproduces naturally only after its own kind. This is contrary to the "origin of the species" and other kindred concepts. These are unproven theories, which were just as unproven from the days of Aristotle to those of Charles Darwin.

During the millennium, the theory of biological evolution will be dispelled and properly left in the trash heap for disproven and discarded theories. One will also notice (in verse 40) that there are at least three major types of orbs in the universe, and that man will resurrect a body capable of living on one of them eternally, depending on his obedience to Celestial, Terrestrial or Telestial Law.

Genesis Creationist Theory and Assumption V

MORTAL BLOOD BROUGHT REPRODUCTION AND DEATH

Book of Genesis

The fall of Adam brought death to earth and all plant and animal forms of life. The most logical explanation for Adam's initiation of a mortal blood supply having a more universal effect is the assumption that God not only permitted Adam the agency to fall, but that God therefore caused the earth to fall, then ceased functioning under Terrestrial Law and all on it to move into a new orbit subject to a Telestial Law. This choice to take the fruit is referred to as the original sin. But it gave the first single couple the power to obey God's commandment to multiply. This power was lacking in their original bodies when they entered Eden. In addition it gave the Lord, (who cannot look upon sin with the least degree of allowance), a way to send all men through the necessary mortal sin experience, without His direct action, to bring that sinful state upon mankind. Originally Adam had a spirit fluid circulating in his vans. It was probably close to the plant chlorophyll, as that is very simular to blood plasma. When he took the forbidden fruit it converted this fluid to mortal blood which has an iron content that plant sap does not have.

Genesis Creationist Theory and Assumption VI

THE GARDEN OF EDEN WAS NOT IN MESOPOTAMIA

Book of Genesis

Even though Noah and his descendants renamed the river Euphrates, the record clearly states that four, not two major rivers joined near the Garden of Eden. The other primary clue to the location of Eden is that Adam's descendant, Noah, at the end of the Adamic Dispensation, at God's direction constructed an Ark of "Gopher Wood". If Eden was on what is now the Western hemisphere it must have been near northern Florida, which had the only source of that type of cypress wood in the Western Hemisphere. There are multiple locations for the growth of that type of cypress in the Eastern hemisphere. The Gopher Wood, the four major rivers and the presence of gold in the land of Havilah are the best clues for the honest seeker of understanding.

Genesis Creationist Theory and Assumption VII

ADAM'S FALL AFFECTED ALL LIFE AND THE EARTH ITSELF

Book of Genesis
Adam's fall was down from a higher terrestrial type state (versus up from the base of a tree). The earth itself fell to a new lesser telestial law type orbit with the sun, moon and stars as we see them today. The results were as follows:

All forms of life on earth became subject to death and received limits to their physical growth. All forms were provided with the power, in this telestial type environment, to reproduce only within their own kind. Mutated variations within a species were in order, but there were to be no cross species or reproduction of new species. Some species were carnivores. This instituted "the law of the jungle" within the animal, fish and fowl worlds.

The animals of the Adamic Dispensation were larger and healthier than those of the same species on the earth today. The flood had not yet reduced the nutritional value of plants and animals growing on the earth's surface. Both animals and men were much stronger, larger and lived longer. See Genesis 5:26 and 6:4. The larger, healthier, stronger species of the Adamic Dispensation may have been required to move quickly to avoid extinction by being eaten by dinosaurs.

The best firm visual proof of these animals is on display at the La Brea Tar Pits. They are located a couple of blocks west of La Brea on the north side of Wilshire Blvd in West Los Angeles, California. Anyone can see for themselves the larger life forms that lived in the Western hemisphere before the flood. The curators of the museum are baffled by the fact that the extinction of these larger species was abrupt and nearly instantaneous. What borders on the hilarious is the avoidance of any mention of the first-hand Bible account of the world enveloping flood and the many questionable ideas suggested, to make what you can see with your eyes, conform to obsolete biological evolutionist theories.

Weeds, disease and pestilence were part of the new fallen environment. The Garden of Eden became a memory and Adam a myth. This meant that the Lord's decree, that man rightly should from that day forth "earn his bread by the sweat of his brow", was made effective.

A second major condition became operable. Man was no longer innocent, but very capable and apt to sin. This added more misery and disease to his condition. Because our first parents were superior in body, virtue and intellect, they read and wrote in a pure Adamic language. Adam and Eve taught their children to read and write, and no doubt to do sums and enjoy music. They were, however, cut off by a veil of memory from their pre-mortal experiences. Nevertheless, the Lord appeared and walked and talked to them and taught them of the atonement and His plan for the resurrection and salvation of all mankind. He taught them, by the eternal growth principle of faith, to sacrifice their best ram each year. After many years of obedient sacrifice they learned from an angel that the sacrifice of the spotless ram was similar to the sacrifice of Jesus Christ in the meridian of time. We, in like manner, are given knowledge from God, after repetitious obedience, to His laws on the principle of faith.

Adam and Eve reproduced, and a Moslem text of Genesis tells us that twins were common. Eve's pain in birthing was much multiplied and was no longer the joyful experience of the premortal sphere. Note: Celestial mothers' birthings are, (we have been told), as joyful as conception. The spirits they give birth to are elastic in nature, therefore multiple birthing is probably common with no currently known upper limit, as to numbers of intelligences clothed with a spirit body in a single birthing.

Another proof of the perfection or (thoroughbred) condition of the bodies of Adam and Eve is that it is obvious that for several generations, brothers and sisters married and birthed healthy children with longevity of life.

A majority of their children used their God-given free choice in youth to leave their innocent, pure and wholesome state to become carnal, sensual and devilish. Jealous Cain murdered Abel because, the Arab text says, he wished to marry his own twin sister versus the twin sister of Abel recommended by Adam and Eve. Rape, the other non-recompensable sin, became common. Castration, creating eunuchs, appears to have been the proper remedy for the rapist. All the lesser and easily repented for sins became prevalent. Adam, knowing that he had brought permanent sin and death on all mankind, was overjoyed when he learned that Jehovah would be sent to attain his mortal condition and atone for the original and all other repented sins. Christ would provide a resurrection of all and forgiveness for the repentant. An Arab text tells us that Adam was so overjoyed that he packaged a gift of gold, frankincense and myrrh and gave it to his descendants to pass down to Noah who would take it to Ararat as a gift for the young Christ child. At Kayseri, Turkey's largest city near Ararat, there stands a monument stating that the wise men of the east met here to go down to find the young Christ child. They presented the gifts to the young Savior at Nazareth, just prior to the need for his parents to flee to Egypt for safety.

The people of the land of Nod were simply a group of Adam and Eve's descendants who had settled in that location. There is no logical justification to use the mention of Nod to suggest a separately created group of people. Each couple who married and lived together created a new family unit. Adam and Eve probably had the birth of one or more children every two or three years. Being productive for about 300 years, with the multiplication of grandchildren each year, proves how foolish it is to worry about the origin of people of Nod. They needed the experience of living independently in a family group for their growth, testing and development on a basis similar to Adam and Eve, the parents of all born in mortality on this earth.

Enjoying free agency, each hearkened to or ignored the teachings of Adam and Eve. Yes, they had their free choice. However, one does not have to be a rocket scientist to understand that, after making it, there are no free but only natural unerring consequences. Unfortunately, the majority became carnal, sensual and devilish as a natural consequence of choosing to ignore Adam's or other parental teaching as to the way of peace and happiness. Murder, lasciviousness, violence and war became the order of the day. Most of Adam's descendants lived and died on the animal plane. Perhaps Jehovah was enjoying his seventh day of rest between Adam and Enoch and permitted these first generations of men to follow their own carnal desires without divine intervention.

A small minority exercised faith, obeyed Adam's teachings of faith, repentance and baptism and obtained the Holy Spirit for their guide. When Jehovah decided that the generation of Adam's descendants of the first millennium were a waste, he determined in His mercy to wipe them off the earth in order that a new generation of children could be reared by a more pure and sensible parentage. He therefore sent Enoch (not the descendant of Cain but the son of Jared) to teach again the foundation principles of His plan of happiness and salvation (i.e. faith, repentance, baptism and the Holy Ghost) in order that all who had chosen to follow God versus Satan should be preserved before the days of Noah and the flood that God was determined to bring upon the earth.

Enoch stood on his land and called all who would repent from among the violent animalistic sons of Adam to gather to the city of Enoch. When all those willing to live by faith in God were so assembled, Jehovah caused the land mass of the city of Enoch (about 3140 B.C.) to be drawn up and fly free from the earth to an orbit separate from earth. Many believe the Gulf of Mexico was created when Enoch's city was taken up, perhaps by joining with another earth type body that passed near the earth. A legendary similar spin-off of territory where the Adriatic Sea is, in about 700 B.C., may have been required to create balance and/or stability in the significantly reduced earth's weight and mass. The earliest maps of the Mediterranean do not show the Adriatic Sea. Perhaps this is the origin of the legend of the Lost Continent of Atlantis. Each of these events would possibly have caused major changes in the placement of earth's orbit and probably other changes on the surface of the earth.

Genesis Creationist Theory and Assumption VIII

THE TOTAL BAPTISM (IMMERSION) OF EARTH BY THE FLOOD

Book of Genesis
Adam and Eve came with more perfect bodies and their food and environment were superior, as attested by the longevity of their lives. Methuselah, the son of Enoch, whose city was caught up, lived to a record 969 years while most born after the flood have to really be well endowed and have proper nutrition to achieve even 120 years.

A logical reason for the drastic change brought on at the time of the flood is as follows:

The earth was flooded from beneath and above for forty days and nights. The water which covered all the then existing mountains by 15 cubits, or about 25 to 30 feet of water, prevailed or remained in place for 150 days. Proof of the depth is revealed in the fact that Noah had to take species of fowl (birds) to be saved in the Ark. An affect of water saturating all earth to a depth of perhaps 50 feet below its surface for 150 days would be the soaking out of all soluble mineral substances into the water for most of the top 50 feet. These elements would sink to the depths of the ocean and this explains why they are no longer readily available. If some of those elements were necessary to health and longevity the future inhabitants of earth would be deprived of them and their lifespan would be shortened considerably. The elements leached into the seas would nourish the fishes, etc. of the seas. Perhaps this explains the improved healthiness of people eating much seafood.

Species that had filled the measure of their creation such as the dinosaurs would not have enjoyed a place on the Ark and would have died suddenly as God intended. The swirling waters would have carried their bodies to deep ravines between the strata, then silt and layers of earth and conglomerate would have covered them to a great depth. The multiple layers of strata over them would greatly confuse latter-day theorists married to a simple single evolutionary theory. The finding of a petrified tree, with axe cuts on it, in Alaska means that current theories of the time required for the petrifaction processes must be re-examined in relation to man's origin on earth.

We should teach children not to mourn over the extinction of dinosaurs or any other species, no longer needed on earth. Out in space, on other developing planets, our Lord maintains a gene pool from which any pre-existing species can be replicated when they are needed to fill the measure of their creation. The presence of earth-like planets in other solar systems has recently been verified by astronomers.

Some have argued that the Ark was not large enough to hold all the basic species on earth today. It was 300 cubits long, meaning between 450 and 600 feet. It was 50 cubits wide, meaning 75 to 100 feet. If using the larger 25–inch sacred cubit, it would have been about the size of two football fields end to end. Since there were three such stories or decks we are talking about a craft with as much space as up to six football fields or 180,000 square feet of floor space.

Assuming that Noah and his sons were reasonable and sensible (as is our Lord Jehovah), they, in gathering say meadow grasses, would plan to feed it to herbivores for about six months. Common sense says that if one intended to feed elephants and shovel their droppings, Noah's sons would not have loaded mature, but baby elephant and other large species pairs.

This was no doubt the way that perhaps the twelve to fifteen largest species were transported on the Ark. Baby pairs of say ten of the largest species would not have required more than about 300 to 600 square feet, with a like amount of space near them, for food storage. Note, for example, that only one pair of dogs was required to parent mutated St. Bernards as poodles. One pair of cats ancestored lions and tabby cats. One pair of carnivore birds would produce variations in that species or family. Seven of each clean animal (primarily non-carnivores) were taken in the Ark to feed Noah's family and the carnivores.

The dinosaurs were probably used by the Lord to create our man-sustaining well-balanced atmosphere. They are with little doubt discussed by Job. He refers to the Behemoth as follows:

> Behold now behemoth, which I made with thee; he eateth grass as an ox. Lo now, his strength is in his loins and his force is in the navel of his belly. He moveth his tail like a cedar: the sinews of his stones are wrapped together. His bones are as strong pieces of brass; his bones are like bars of iron. He is the chief of the ways of God: he that made him can make his sword to approach unto him. Surely the mountains bring him forth food, where all the beasts of the field play. He lieth under the shady trees, in the covert of the reed and fens. The shady trees cover him with their shadow; the willows of the brook compass him about. Behold he drinketh up a river, and hasteth not; he trusteth that he can draw up the Jordan into his mouth. He taketh it with his eyes; his nose pierceth through snares.
>
> Job 40:15–24

In viewing nearly all dinosaurs, it is noted that they are very heavy in the loins. Their tails resemble tree trunks. Their bulk make them the chief of God's creations in size. Such an animal would appear to drink up a river.

The mention of the Jordan would at first glance appear to indicate a late date for the Book of Job. However, the tendencies to repeat names of rivers used to rename new rivers, etc., during the migrations of men is a ready explanation. Because Noah lived 950 years, he was still living when Abraham was born. Job, most probably never saw a living dinosaur. He could have seen them drowned and made extinct by God's will in the universal flood. Nevertheless, he would have learned about them from Noah and his family, who lived before the universal flood.

Creationist Theory and Assumption IX

THE ICE AGE AND OTHER CATACLYSMS REFUTE EVOLUTIONIST DATING

Book of Genesis
The major Ice Age was the natural result in (polar climes) of the cooling of the earth's total atmosphere due to evaporation. The evaporation which cooled water in the horse farmers canvas water bag explains what happened to the earth after the flood had soaked down over 100 feet from the surface of the earth during the universal worldwide flood and the ice age that naturally followed through evaporation. As the total land mass of the earth emerged after the flood, which baptized or totally immersed it, the natural evaporation brought about a total drop in temperature that created massive ice packs. The rapid disappearance of glaciers upsets current multiple Ice Age theories and leads to questionable global warming concepts. Might it be suggested that there was but one Ice Age about 4,400 years ago, and that the melt has been fairly even and continuous with cycles created by the weather patterns from year to year.

The land of Enoch (and later perhaps the Adriatic) being carried into space plus the flood and the Ice Age had an effect on the basic orbit and atmosphere of the earth, as attested by an apparently new phenomenon, the sighting of rainbows. The once paradisiacal land now required periodic rain and snow to carry moisture to areas now orbiting in dryer latitudes. To get a clearer picture of the impact of these rapidly sequenced cataclysms, read the scholarly but censored (by scholastics and book publishers) meticulously researched books of Immanuel Velikovsky. The extent of the censorship can be realized by reading his *Stargazers and Gravediggers*. To sense the impact of these early cataclysms see his *Earth in Upheaval* and *Ages in Chaos* bravely published by Doubleday. The "scholarly censorship" has been so effective that obtaining the works of this author is in most cases limited to inter-library loan. Velikovsky held seven "earned versus honorary" doctorates and wrote a book for each thesis.

The effects of this massive Ice Age are quite evident and observable in many locations on earth such as the northern border of the U.S.A. from North Dakota to Maine.

To restore faith in the Bible chronology versus Egyptology and profane scholastic history, study the scrupulously researched writings of Immanuel Velikovsky. His research verifies the Bible chronology with only a slight mention of the Bible.

The student of the scriptures desiring guidance in their last days should diligently study Isaiah. Over 2,730 years ago Isaiah spoke clearly of the humble birth and ministry of the Savior and foretold the events prior to His Second Coming in power to rule the earth for a celestial day as 1,000 years. We should not be too judgmental of the Jews during Christ's ministry. Had we lived at that time, the records of a sweet humble Messiah may have been confusing to us. Especially when the same Isaiah speaks of the great Messiah coming to power. Careful study of Isaiah 29 reveals that in the last days the "Wisdom of the wise shall perish". It is our hope that this work will aid in that process. Our children should learn and cleave to truth instead of becoming slaves to repetitious detrimental theories.

To those concerned with the chasm between the scriptorian and the secular scholar it appears that Immanuel Velikovsky's works are the harbingers of the fulfillment of Isaiah's prophecy on worldly wisdom. Velikovsky was the son of an early immigrant from Russia to the Holy Land following the Balfour Declaration. That declaration was given over half a century after the 1840 Orson Hyde proclamation of the return of the Jews to the Holy Land. This Russian Jewish family had such regard for proper education (which is one of the few things that outlasts the grave) that Immanuel *earned* seven (versus honorary) PhDs. He was contemporary and had a close association with both Freud and Einstein. The *Reader's Digest* reported that the day Einstein died, in 1955, one of Velikovsky's books was open on his desk.

Then Einstein said, in substance, "We've got to give more

credence to the work of Velikovsky." The scholastic world, which has fought strenuously against censorship of four-letter words (which crudify our lives), has fought tooth and nail to censor the works of Velikovsky, which can elevate our self-image. Pressure was put on publishing houses to cease publication and college bookstores have refused to carry his well-documented writings. There is a book by ten scientists in opposition to his works. It is a collection of generalities that in substance say, "You can't play in our ball park because you won't follow our well-established theories and rules." A second book by ten scientists lists specific ways in which Velikovsky's excellent research and analysis, when generally understood and accepted, will require changes in nearly every scholastic discipline more theoretical than mathematics.

Early Egyptian historians added 800 to 1,000 years to the chronology of the Egyptians by erroneously listing given dynasties more than once. They listed chronologically the Egyptian-named dynasties, then included the dynasty names used by neighboring peoples. See many proofs given in books by Immanuel Velikovsky. For example in his *Ramses II* he proves that Ramses II was at the battle of Carmack just before 600 B.C. instead of near Moses' time (per Cecil B. DeMille). The first pharaoh of Egypt was after 2400 B.C. versus 3200 B.C. Velikovsky's works are heavy, well documented reading and, due to censorship, very hard to obtain. This scholastic censorship requires most students desiring Velikovsky's books to get them via inter-library loan. When the demand is great enough, his books will be republished and become readily available to foster more sensible discussions and education. His first book was published in 1950 and he died in 1979. A list of his books of which we are aware, with some descriptive comments, is given at the end of this book.

Creationist Theory and Assumption X

CATACLYSMIC EARTH PLATE SEPARATION AND TRIBAL SEPARATION

Book of Genesis

About 2300 B.C. or about 200 years after the flood, Jehovah used his superior intelligence and understanding of the make-up of the earth he had created under the direction of His Father Elohim to, in the days of Peleg, divide the earth. The crust plates that previously formed the band of the sub-tropical paradisiacal preflood earth were now thrust apart very rapidly, creating from the one single band of earth seven major continental areas, if Greenland is included. In addition, there were multitudinous islands of the oceans and inland lakes created in the spreading process. There is no detailed recorded account of the impact on mankind of these turbulent days. This rapid division of the earth in the days of Peleg, followed by the scattering and division of the families of mankind, were part of God's plan. High winds brought down the tower of Babel in about 2200 B.C. and again mankind scrambled for life and suffered a stupor of thought. See *Mankind in Amnesia* by Velikovsky.

Asia was the largest subcontinent into which the tribes of Japheth were driven as they migrated to the north and southeast of the Caspian Sea. Ham's grandson, Nimrod the mighty hunter, founded Babel, Erech and Acled, and also Calmeth in the land of Shinar. Nimrod was the ruler of Mesopotamia who raised the tower of Babel. Most of Ham's descendents were driven westward to the lower Nile River delta. They named the area Egypt in honor of Egyptus, the wife of Ham. Their eldest son, named Pharaoh, was the first king of Egypt. Later rulers were referred to as the Pharaohs. In this post-Babel period snakes infested the land of Egypt and many parts of the earth. Various groups of Ham's descendants pushed west along the borders of the Mediterranean, also south up the Nile and into the interior of Africa, creating civilizations that would later be driven further south with the encroachment of the Sahara Desert. Canaan, son of Ham, and his bands settled in what is now the Holy Land. Their remnants, like those who followed the Mediterranean shores westward, were wiped out or inter-married with various tribes of Shem. Descendants of Shem pushed west and northwest, while descendants of Japheth pushed eastward and also northeast and southeast.

Creationist Theory and Assumption XI

NOAH'S SONS SEPARATE, CHOSEN HEBREW RACE COMES FROM SHEM

Book of Genesis

Noah's movements within or from Mesopotamia are not mentioned. Therefore, it is assumed he remained and was nurtured in that land by Shem and his family who stayed in Mesopotamia but whose clans pushed westward into Canaan and Phoenicia and northwest into Asia Minor, Istanbul, Greece, Rome, Spain, Northern Europe, Britain and Scandinavia.

Noah, his sons, and their wives transitioned from the Adamic pre-flood world to the Noachian post-flood dispensation. Their genetic make-up was such that they lived longer lives than their post-flood descendants, who lived to about 120 years probably because of the depletion of nutrients on the surface of the earth caused by the flood. Noah lived 950 years and had lived only nineteen years less than Methuselah.

Uz was a grandson of Noah and his clans pushed westward across the Arabian Desert. His people settled, probably along the Arar River and the lake it runs into, in central Arabia and westward to border against Moab and or Edom. Job lived in the land of Uz and the book of Job is therefore preceded chronologically only by the book of Genesis recording the lives of earlier patriarchs.

The Bible history gives more detail on the lives of the descendants of Shem than on Japheth or Ham. Shem's sons were Elam, Asshur, Arphaxad, Lud and Aram, the father of Uz. Shem's great-grandson through Arphazad was Eber, Father of Hebrews and of Peleg down through Nahor and Terah to Abraham.

With the birth of Abraham in about 2123 B.C., a new dispensation from heaven was to begin. Abraham was about 127 years old when his faith was tested on Mt. Moriah. Having passed the test, he became the Father of the Faithful—the Father of those destined by their ability to, by faith, obey the Lord's directions in areas not always open to physical sight and understanding. Nevertheless, these few would have the quality of faith needed to facilitate and cause them to grow and develop in obedience to God and became Celestial beings in the resurrection.

Only those understanding and willing to put themselves in harmony with the laws of the Celestial Kingdom will mature into full Godhead and become joint heirs of that kingdom with Jehovah/Jesus Christ. All others will reside in lesser kingdoms of glory.

Famine forced Abraham to go to Egypt for survival. It is probable that Abraham, having advanced knowledge of astronomy from the early patriarchal fathers, shared it with the Egyptians. Abraham's intelligence from God, related to astronomy, is the likely source of the advanced intelligence of Egypt. Sarah's beauty is attested by the fact that both Pharaoh and Abimelech desired her. Abraham's telling them that she was his sister is a fact. The kings probably did not understand that, when born as spirit bodies to heavenly resurrected parents, all men and women are brothers and sisters.

Abraham, led by the Lord, was given the Holy Land as a home for his descendants. But, as recorded in Genesis, his immediate descendants, Isaac, Jacob and Joseph first migrated to Egypt to raise livestock in the Land of Goshen. However, they would become slaves to the Egyptians for four generations. Jehovah promised Abraham after he rescued Lot in about 1974 B.C. that his descendants would return from Egyptian slavery in 400 years.

Jacob's new name given him by God was Israel. In Egypt he blessed each of his sons and the two sons of Joseph (see Genesis Ch. 48–49). The most significant and relatively easily understood of these prophetic blessings were first Joseph's, a double portion including him and his sons Ephraim and Manasseh. Israel gave the greatest blessing to Ephraim including the birthright he would use to bless all of Israel, including his elder brother Manasseh.

Joseph's personal blessing affecting his descendants indicates that they would be as the branches of a fruitful bough, which would at a later date, run over a wall (water barrier) to inhabit the Western hemisphere. Yes, some Mongolians did cross over to Alaska as proven by the Mongoloid dark spot at the base of the spine of some Eskimo tribes. However this hereditary spot is not in sufficient evidence in Native American tribes south of Alaska. This puts the theory of the primary population of the western hemisphere from Mongolia in question. Native Americans kept a stick or record of the dealing of Jehovah's dealings with them. The records of Judah and Joseph spoken of by Ezekiel 37:15–17 was a reminder of actions required of the Lord at the time that Joseph went over the wall. The unicorn is the symbol of the tribe of Ephraim or Joseph. Unicorns will return with the lost tribes of the house of Israel in later days (see Isaiah 34:7). Archeologists who lack understanding of this scripturally recorded migration operate under a severe handicap.

Judah's blessing was the other blessing and prophecy to have a major impact. Judah would enjoy the good things of earth, including wealth and the power of the kingly class.

His sons would be the kings of the earth and the scepter bearers should not depart from beneath his loins or feet until Shiloh or Christ should come (the Second Coming) is inferred. The lion is the symbol of the tribe of Judah. It should be noted that half of the tribe of Benjamin became Jewish and that many of the tribe of Levi, previously scattered among the tribes, may have migrated to Judah just before the ten and a half tribes were captured, then escaped and became "lost". You will note that there are a total of thirteen tribes. When Joseph received a double portion thirteen tribes were created. However, because Levi was scattered to all tribes as spiritual leaders with no tribal area assigned, the number is again twelve. For lack of cohesiveness and a designated land inheritance, Levite blood continues in all tribes but Levi is not listed in the twelve. The Jewish tribe or race originated when the ten tribes of Israel became lost. Jews do not include all of Israel but just two and a half tribes of Israel.

The next two blessings appear a bit more clear and pre-eminent than the balance which are either sufficiently clear or so obscure that they will not be discussed here but should be studied by students of the Bible.

Dan's blessing indicates a heritage of expansion and adventure, probably as Norsemen, in key areas of the earth while at the same time they indicate a sea gate control of narrow straits over the earth that have been used to regulate other nations' shipping via the allegory of the horse and rider. Denmark appears to be the home of many of the children of Dan. Many others went by sea to other areas such as Ireland. Descendants of Dan have blessed the world with a democratic, less kingly leadership. They have helped guide the rest of mankind through many rough shoals.

Zebulun will be a seafaring people. The haven of ships suggests quiet harbors able to berth an armada. It has been suggested that the Dutch are of Zebulun. The Basque people who live in northern Spain and along the French border in the Pyrenees Mountains claim to be a chosen people. Before they became famous as shepherds they were seamen of renown. Marco Polo was a Spanish Basque. Could they be of Zebulun?

In summary, each inhabitant of the earth enjoys four or more common "Fathers":

1. We are all literal spirit children of Elohim or God the Father and our Celestial Mother. They are both resurrected beings who attained godhead status and will parent spirit children eternally.
2. Jehovah, by coming to earth as the Christ to atone for all and make forgiveness and our resurrection possible, becomes the Father of our resurrected bodies. He also becomes Father to those willing to obey and follow Him. He is the father of all earth's resurrected bodies.
3. Adam and Eve were the original parents of all mortal men assigned to this earth.
4. Since Noah is, also the common progenitor of all men born after the flood, he and his wife are common parents to all.
5. Our earthly parents made it possible for us to advance from a spirit world existence into the mortal bodies we now enjoy. Joseph is the common father of all who came primarily from the tribes of Ephraim or Manasseh.
    Branches of Ephraim and Manasseh went over the ocean "wall" to populate and inhabit the western hemisphere. See Genesis 49:22-26.

Creationist Theory and Assumption XII

JOB'S CLUES TO MAN'S ORIGIN, LIFE'S PURPOSE AND ETERNAL DESTINY

Book of Job

Chronologically the book of Job comes from the time of the patriarchs. He lived in the land of Uz east of Moab. Uz was a grandson of Noah and the name is later used in the days of Esau. One of the first things we learn from Job is that Satan, an advanced spirit, early on had access to God's presence. Satan is a real person who is damned within a body of spirit, and the book of Job is historical versus allegorical. It is imperative that we understand that Satan and his unseen forces work tirelessly with their fiery darts of temptation to entice us to leave the high road leading to God and eternal happiness, to follow Satan and his host and thus reap eternal damnation and sorrow. The book of Job enjoys the power to cause the student to ponder the purposes and the natural laws applicable to each man being tested by God in the mortal life. We learn in the thirty-seventh chapter of Job that all natural laws of this sphere were instituted by God.

God has a plan and a prescribed course for our success and happiness in life. It is up to us to recognize that it is a "do-ityourself" course obtained only by our prayer, scripture study, search and obedience based at first on the principle of faith. The truth has been restored to earth and it is up to each of us to find it, embrace it, and get in harmony with Celestial law if we desire and work for Celestial rewards. The book of Job causes us to recognize our own ignorance and that we need answers to many questions. For instance, the thirty-eighth chapter causes us to recognize our lack of understanding about how the earth was organized (created). Also to wonder where we were at that time when the morning stars sang together and all the sons of God shouted for joy. This hints that we were there and may have, under Jehovah's direction, assisted in the formation of the earth for our further development and progress.

When Jesus said, "Before Abraham, I am...", he was testifying his pre-mortal existence as the Jehovah of the Old Testament. When Jehovah said to Jeremiah, "Before I formed thee in the belly I knew thee and before thou comest out of the womb I sanctified thee and ordained thee a prophet unto the nations," it appears to be a safe assumption that God is telling mankind that they and their prophets enjoyed a pre-mortal life. In other words, we all lived as spirits before our mortality. Since it says in Job "all the sons of God", it can also be assumed that we were together rejoicing at the formation of the earth a minimum of 13,000 years ago.

We are equal in God's love, mercy and justice. It does not follow that all are equal at birth. The reason for this is easy to understand. God has protected our agency and free choice of our course in life not only in mortality but in the pre-mortal spirit state, and as eternally existing intelligences prior to our birth to heavenly parents in spirit bodies. Each day of our pre-mortal lives we, through diligence and obedience or carefree disobedience and sloth, charted our ongoing rate of development. Just as peers' progress at different rates here, so it was in pre-mortality. Today's proper or improper use of our agency to progress toward perfection determines our future destiny. Just as men resurrect to different heavenly rewards, so our time and condition of birth are determined by our pre-mortal progress. See Acts 17:26. We can assume that our loving Heavenly Father places each spirit in the most favorable circumstances that his or her pre-mortal performance has entitled them to.

Additional proofs of these truths are testified by two or more witnesses per John 8:17 and I Timothy 5:19 in the following references: John 1:1–14, 8:57, I Peter 1:19–20, Ecclesiastes 12:7, John 9:1–2, Ephesians 1:3–6, Hebrews 12:9, Revelation 12:7–12, Jude 6.

In summary, there are many additional scriptures that suggest or clarify the truths that can be obtained based on sound creationist theories. However, the books of Genesis and Job appear pre-eminent in their ability to help us understand how and, of more importance, why this earth was created, its purposes, its laws, and our missions upon it. They also answer life's most basic questions. In Joseph's life we see that the basic tests of all mankind are industry, honesty and virtue. Genesis and Job reveal unto us where we come from and what the purpose of our life's quest is. They also reveal what the possible destinies are or what our individual eternal destiny is. Additionally, these creationist theories and assumptions obtained via faith and reading of the scriptural revelations from God are more than adequate to be measured against and compete in the marketplace with the theory of evolution.

There is nothing one can see that has not at some time been created (organized) by an intelligent personage. To accept this fact is certainly more rational than accepting a scheme where all the orderly complex relationships are supposed to have fallen in place by chance.

Creationist Theory and Assumption XIII

EGYPT SAVED BY HEBREWS, SLAVERY THEIR REWARD THEN FREED BY JEHOVAH

Book of Exodus

Prior to Moses' time the Egyptians grew fearful of the growing strength of Israelite tribes as they prospered in the Land of Goshen. It is ironic that they made slaves of the Israelites who had saved them from drought. The Egyptians forced them to build cities and pyramids after Joseph, at God's direction, had insured survival of Egypt. It is even more ironic that Israel was forced to build pyramids that have proven to be in delicate astrological alignment when the Egyptians had gained that knowledge from an earlier drought-driven visit of Abraham to Egypt.

Before the exodus and entry into the Holy Land the Israelites were the pyramid builders of Egypt. See Genesis 49:22 and Ezekiel 37:15–28. Some of the descendants of the Israelites, shipped over the wall of the Pacific Ocean to ride the counterequatorial current, disembarked probably in Northern Chile. It is a reasonable assumption that they created the pyramids of Central and South America that stand as proof that the skill to build them existed in both hemispheres.

Creationist Theory and Assumption XIV

THE PROPONENTS OF THE THEORY OF EVOLUTION WILL MEET THE CREATOR AT THE FINAL JUDGMENT

It's time for those who have had faith and have come to know our loving Father in Heaven to take the attitude that those who have made a religion of biological evolution do not exist. The reasoning behind this is really quite simple. Those foolish enough to believe that life originated by chance, spontaneous generation or a lightning bolt into a mud soup are really saying "we do not have, nor need a creator".

Our response is simple and straightforward: "If you were not created by a loving, intelligent creator, you simply do not exist!"

As a matter of history, Cain ignored the law of his parents and his God. Since that time, in every generation, those who desire to be a law unto themselves stress their free choice and their right to ignore God's laws.

The "free choicers" rail against the God-fearing with accusations that they don't understand free choice. Sadly, the ignorance is on the part of the "free choicers" who say, "I'll make my free choice and all is well." They are poor misguided souls worthy of our compassion for the sorrows of life have not taught them a more basic truth. Irremovably attached to every choice, free or otherwise, is the natural consequence of that choice. There are some so blind that they feel they can act sinfully, rudely or maliciously and not have a serious price to pay.

There is no such thing as free choice because there are good or bad natural consequences to each choice. We are, however, free to choose truth, freedom and happiness or misery and lies.

Creationist Theory and Assumption XV

THE SUN STANDS STILL—EARTH'S ORBIT TURNS ELLIPTICAL

Book of Joshua

There are a lot of miracles spoken of in the Book of Exodus. The ten plagues of Egypt, snakes and staffs and rods that bend; food for nearly two million people and their livestock miraculously provided as manna; the appearance of doves in the wilderness; water provided or purified simplistically without expensive modern equipment; water brought forth with the strike of a staff and earthquakes that split the earth in the correct location to swallow the disobedient.

How did Moses do it? We just don't know. But we do know that Moses was the ear and Aaron the mouthpiece of the Lord to the people. A concept from the Hebrew Torah or Law, which was not translated into Christian Bibles, is that of the Shechinah— meaning fire, light, smoke or other signs to the people, that God was present with his selected, prepared and appointed prophets. Light and non-consuming fire are the most prevalent signs of the Shechinah.

Because of his most singular and thorough research, searchers should be able to ponder and enjoy the writings of Immanuel Velikovsky. His *Worlds in Collision was* drawn from the myths all around the world. It gives some of Velikovsky's rather natural explanations for much of the miraculous in the Book of Exodus. Old star maps prove that Venus orbited outside the earth from the sun in early times. From the time of Moses, Venus's orbit is shown between the sun and the earth. Velikovsky points out that Mars came close to the earth in about 700 B.C. and that a legendary land mass was drawn from the earth, possibly creating the Adriatic and causing theGreeks to proliferate legends of erratic gods acting on earth in varied myths and stories with hidden meanings. Is it not reasonable to ask if people were caught up with the land mass?

Sigmund Freud cast his myth of the universality of the Oedipus complex in all men at Thebes in Greece. See *Oedipus and Akhnaton* by Velikovsky and learn of the true story of a young king who had his mother as his queen at Thebes in Egypt in about 1600 B.C. See in addition that Freud suffered from the Oedipus complex that he tried to attribute to all men. Like many others living by the light of their own candle, Freud lacked faith in God and his prophets. He attributed moral grossness to Moses, which caused him to faint when he saw Michelangelo's Moses pointing at him from the ceiling of the Sistine Chapel.

In Joshua 10:12–14 and in the Book of Jasher, there are accounts of the Lord causing the sun to appear to stand still while Joshua gave the Amorites their comeuppance. Without throwing all men from the earth by halting its rotation, the most logical assumption is that the earth made an orbital ellipse in its forward rotation that made the sun appear to stand still. That ellipse would have required a change of the earth's axis. Tropical flora and fauna frozen in Alaskan and Siberian tundra prove that the earth's axis has moved. On earth we find the evidence with semitropical flora and fauna being found encased in the frozen tundra of Alaska and Siberia. The petrified tropical trees found in Northern Arizona further testify to changes in earth's polarity. The searcher should read Velikovsky's most scholarly and scientific works, *Earth in Upheaval.* Primitive educators censored his books but a clamor is being raised by requests of those who wish to study his unparalleled research and insights. It is probable that the sun's ten-degree transgression and regression spoken of in Isaiah 38:8 and II Kings 20:9–10 did not affect the earth as drastically as the sun standing still, in the days of Joshua.

King Hezekiah requested a sign from God that the Lord would prolong his life 15 years. It was granted, and the more difficult retrograde of the sundial shadow 10% or about 40 minutes took place 730 B.C.

This event was verified by secular witnesses. The Grecian Herodotus, "Father of History", discussed it, quoting from records shown to him while he was a priest in Egypt. Also the Chinese Emperor Yew, who lived in Joshua's day.

Creationist Theory and Assumption XVI

SIGNS OF CHRIST'S THREE DAY RESURRECTION—NINEVEH REPENTS

Book of Jonah

Many have poked fun at and have derided the story of Jonah. They call it a myth or an allegory. They fail to recognize that Jonah was not necessarily swallowed by a whale "but by a large fish prepared by the Lord". A fish not a mammal is what the Book of Jonah states. This means that a completely different digestive system was involved. However, that is only a minor point in the story. The important lesson for us to learn is that, if by God or His authority through a prophet, we are given a mission or task from God we had best carry it out as He would have us do. Jonah had to learn that "they that do the Lord's work, get the Lord's pay". However, one must carry out God's will when special personal tasks are assigned. Oddly, the Babylonians repented and saved themselves. In addition they were prepared to host the Jewish captives who would start living among them about 188 years later.

As one reads the Old Testament it is hard to ignore the parallel stories of the scripture and their replication in the Hellenistic stories of the Iliad and the Odyssey attributed to Homer. Review Judges 4:18–24 for the similarity of the story of the Cyclops. The parallel is a bit vague. However, there cannot be any mistaking of the relationship between Judges 6:36–40 and the Greek story of Jason and the Golden Fleece. Alexander the Great it was claimed was of virgin birth and the son of one of the gods of Mt. Olympus. Prophetic as the legend appears, it is best to assume he was fathered by one-eyed Phillip of Macedonia. This myth about Alexander does provide a prophecy relative to Christ's birth. The Godhead of the Bible are role models for mankind, while the Greek gods evolving from Greek myths (sometimes carrying certain truths) are man-made gods that have all the vices and weaknesses of men. One of the signs of Christ crucifixion was three days of total darkness on the western hemisphere.

Creationist Theory and Assumption XVII

JEHOVAH BORN AS JESUS CHRIST, AND HIS CRUCIFIXION BRINGS ABOUT THE SALVATION OF MAN AND EARTH

The Gospels

When Jehovah, the Creator of heaven and earth, was born as Jesus Christ in Bethlehem, many astronomical and earth-shaking events took place. Guiding stars in the heavens, the stilling of the waves about to swamp the Apostles' ship in the Sea of Galilee demonstrated his Godly power. The thunder, lightning, earthquakes and darkness that accompanied His death on the Cross show that all creation responded to the death of the Creator.

In life He spoke of other sheep he must visit and there is in the Book of III Nephi, Chapters 8–28, the record of the cataclysmic forces working on the earth from his Crucifixion until he had finished his ministry in the Western hemisphere. At his Crucifixion the entire face of the land of the Western hemisphere was changed. Besides III Nephi Chapter 8, searchers for truth should review the implications of the Washoe Indian Legend recorded in Chapter XVIII and *A Marvelous Work and A Wonder* by Legrand Richards.

When one sees the havoc created by Lake Bonneville's breaking through Red Rock Pass at that time (it not only lowered Lake Bonneville by 300 feet but tore up the southeastern portion of Idaho for 200 miles in its rush down to the channel of the Snake River), the final or summary assumption is that each major event testified to in the scripture which caused cataclysmic changes over the earth testifies to the rapidly changed conditions we see upon the face of the whole earth.

The theory of evolution is just that, an unproven theory. Mutation within a species is a proven fact, but as any species mutates to the boundaries of its given species the offspring are infertile. Examples are the mule and the extensive research performed on fruit flies. Too often the fact of species mutation gets confused with the theories of biological evolution. Evolution from one species to another has never been demonstrated but is based on multitudinous assumptions and repetitious willful thinking. Its only strength is the monotonous repetition of the theory, supported now by college professors who were duped in the second grade of their scholastic life. They are either afraid or too unmotivated to seriously question the rot they perpetuate. It's easier to never rock the boat and to just repeat unsound theory by rote while enjoying a respected station in life.

They appear to want a system that they hope will not require them to be weighed in a final judgment by a living God. They refuse to understand His word, especially relative to the Genesis revelation that each species must reproduce "after its kind". Although mutations occur they have never demonstrated a living evolution. Like chance crap shooters they just keep juggling the bones to fit acceptable theories. They ignore the fact that Jehovah through Noah used the Ark to preserve all the species that had not yet filled the measure of their creation. The "one size fits all" evolutionary cult dogma gives unsuspecting grade school students the idea that man has evolved from a simple life form in an unending upward advance. Today's society, in all its decadence, is convinced that it is the most advanced society in the universe. Pride goeth before destruction and a haughty spirit before a fall, Proverbs 16:18.

The truth is that Adam, and his family, were probably more intelligent and healthy than us, with all our medical advances. The course of history, from Adam to the present day, has not been one upward plane of progress. Instead, it has been a series of ups and downs, light and darkness depending on man's obedience or disobedience to God's laws. Each major new dispensation prophet, verified to his followers by the Shechinah light, has restored the eight basic principles for successful living. In each case for about 200 years society enjoyed a renewal and return to ealthy progress on an upward plane. Unfortunately, after a couple of centuries the majority begin misusing their freedom of choice to become carnal, sensual and devilish. This creates a distinct decline and degeneration of body, mind and spirit. After the better part of a millennium, degeneration brought an age of darkness before Jehovah sent another major prophet to initiate renewal in a restoration dispensation. The Old Greeks, not Darwin, first taught and relied on the theory of biological evolution. It was so unprovable that it was a dead issue until Darwin thought to resurrect it.

During the age of darkness, in a return to primitive conditions, various clans became cavemen, Cro-Magnon or other degenerate species of mankind. So we do not have a single upward plane of progress, but a series of peaks and valleys, ups and downs in human progress or regression. An honest look at archeology and history, both secular and scriptural, witnesses to the validity and truth of this concept. Plainly stated, mankind from Adam onwards has not been on an upward evolutionary journey, but has risen or fallen according to its obedience or disobedience to correct principles for the living taught by Jehovah.

An example of the foolishness perpetuated to support the sacred geological evolutionary theory, made feasible to second graders, required constancy or no change in western United States earth's surface for six billion years or more. Counting strata layers down to the bottom of the Grand Canyon, cut by waters from the Teton's provides a supposed "earth's origin date" used as a sacred trump card by most evolutionists. Proven and demonstrable mutation of species confuses the equation. However, the biological evolution of new species has never been demonstrated beyond logical and reasonable challenges of each supporting theory. Only by monotonous repetition has the theory of evolution been perpetuated. The perfection of carbon dating reduced the Ice Age from 60,000 to 6,000 years B.C. during the author's short lifetime. (The informed divide most current estimate figures by two.) The constantly unaltered earth surface theory is most effectively refuted by eminent researcher and companion of Einstein, Immanuel Velikovsky in his *Earth inUpheaval.* His writing proves we had several cataclysmic earth surface changes during our 6,000-year first-hand historical record. Evolutionists, faithful to their religion, make glib recitations of supposed ages. They fail to recognize that a stable unchanged earth surface must therefore have prevailed over the

U.S. intermountain region for 6 billion years. Since none of us "Vas you Dere Charlie?", let's look at a new theory for the origin of the Grand Canyon. The Big Bang is a bummer, when one knows that our loving anthropomorphic Father in Heaven created (organized) earth from eternally existing matter by rolling strata on strata as one would roll a snowman. The Big Bang theory ignores God's management of matter. It does, however, fit in with the gospel of evolution. The most recent thing astronomers can't account for is the recent discovery of some apparently "newly organized" orbs, which they are calling "brown dwarfs". The rocks on this earth are not only old, but eternal. Accepted science has admitted that matter cannot be destroyed. It can be changed to energy and perhaps vice versa.

Note: we must start admitting that the evolutionary theory is not a proven science. It is a religion as opposed to a science. See *Evolution, Is it Science or Faith?* by the well-known author and renowned lawyer, Jerome Horowitz.

Creationist Theory and Assumption XVIII
ASTEROID CATACLYSMS AT
CHRIST'S CRUCIFIXION

True science, like true religion, will willingly and honestly address all items of evidence, regardless of the source, without prejudice. Unfortunately, scholastics and so-called scientists consistently ignore the firsthand written evidence of the Bible in a less than scientific method of refuting it.

The scholastics tell us that the unicorn is a mythical beast. However, the Lord, through Isaiah, informs us they will return with the lost tribes of Israel in the end time.

> The sword of the Lord is filled with blood, it is made fat with fatness, and with the blood of lambs and goats, with the fat of the kidneys of rams; for the Lord hath a sacrifice in Bozrah, and a great slaughter in the land of Idumea. And the unicorns shall come down with them, and the bullocks with their bulls; and their land shall be soaked with blood, and their dust made fat with fatness. For it is the day of the Lord's vengeance, and the year of recompenses for the controversy of Zion.
>
> Isaiah 34:6–8

During 1997 the author awoke one morning with this question in mind—What really did cause the formation of the continental divide and the other mountain chains that form a baseball diamond box around the Grand Canyon as if that deep hole were the pitcher's mound?

A recent television program had indicated that an asteroid had landed in what is now the Gulf of Mexico. It created a 100-mile implosion crater eighty percent of which is covered by Gulf waters.

A speculated, extremely distant past date was given as a scientific WAG (Wild "Donkey" Guess). One wonders, however, if it had caused the dark mists evident prior to Quetzalcoatl's appearance in Mexico in about A.D. 33. Also did it play a part in the formation of the Copper Canyon, Mexico's larger Grand Canyon? Under sea cities, thought to be Atlantis, were most probably sunken beneath the sea in the Gulf of Mexico, by that asteroid.

Did an asteroid from the west break through the earth's crust shortly after the flood or Ice Age to slosh the magma in such a way that the Continental Divide, the Uintas, Mogollon Mountains and other back splash or ripple west side ranges suddenly created the ball-diamond shape of mountains enclosing the Grand Canyon? The diamond-shaped mountainous lip thrusts of the earth's crust covered with ocean water would have been elevated near Denver, Colorado, as 2nd base end being nearly two miles high, about twenty miles west of Denver. The 1st base, to the south of Gallup, New Mexico, was raised about 1¾ miles high, and going northwest along the Maggollian range it was raised about 1¾ miles. A second 1¾ mile high Uinta range (the only true east–west range in the United States ending at Provo, Utah), as 3rd base, with 700 miles of ocean between 1st and 3rd base (also 2nd and home) rushing waters perhaps two miles deep toward the center of the Grand Canyon (or pitcher's mound), and the whole being raised 14,000 feet at the east or Denver side of the diamond, with the home base near Overton. Nevada remained stable at about 1,200 feet above current sea level.

To clarify, try to see it as a great butterfly with 700 miles between the upthrust wing tips—Provo at one tip and south of Gallup at the other. The center line of that earth's crust would have been cracked by the center line rubble several miles wide and two miles deep. This is very similar to the weakening in paper when one folds it and crosses fold. The head of the butterfly near Denver, with the whole body also elevated about two miles. Now, see it happening during Christ's Crucifixion, as a great oceancovered baseball diamond. Home base at Overton, Nevada, first base, south of Gallup, second base the two 14,000 feet high peaks west of Denver, and third near Provo with the center of the Grand Canyon being the pitcher's fold line or rubble mound. If the land covered by some water was at a 1,200 foot elevation at Logandale, Nevada as home base remained unchanged, the water at Denver (or second base) would be raised two miles when the Continental Divide raised up two miles and forced all the water trapped in the baseball diamond, covering over 160,000 square miles, to be funneled forcefully to the central pitcher's mound, washing out rubble to a depth of 6000 ft. from the north rim to the river. Since bases one and three were also thrust up at the same time, that massive deluge would have flushed all Grand Canyon rubble into the Sea of Cortez in a matter of hours.

The author reasoned that quite possibly the Grand Canyon's origin was the effect of an asteroid striking about 200 miles southwest of Cedar City, Utah. This would be an intelligently aimed asteroid which with cataclysmic force created the canyon in a matter of hours versus eons. Four days after envisioning this theory, the U.S. Geological survey on October 20, 1997, released the finding of an asteroid strike leaving a 120-mile diameter implosion crater between Cedar City, Utah, and Beatty, Nevada. (Don't be confused by theoretical pros and cons but fax USCS for verification of this strike at 303–236–5882.) Evolutionists faithfully tend to ignore any evidence not fitting their theory. It struck just exactly where it would have been required to carry out the actions of the envisioned theory.

The following two western hemisphere witnesses appear to be describing cataclysmic events quite possibly triggered by asteroid strikes at the time of Christ's Crucifixion.

Nephi's Testimony

Now read an account of the Yucatan asteroid, as related in Third Nephi, and you will note that the two accounts agree on practically every detail, even to the length of time in which the sun failed to come up. This is the account given by Nephi of the happenings upon the American continent at the time the Savior was crucified:

> But behold, there was a more great and terrible destruction in the land northward; for behold, the whole face of the land was changed, because of the tempest and the whirlwinds, and the thunderings and

the lightnings, and the exceeding great quaking of the whole earth;

And the highways were broken up, and the level roads were spoiled, and many smooth places became rough.

And many great and notable cities were sunk, and many were burned, and many were shaken till the buildings thereof had fallen to the earth, and the inhabitants thereof were slain, and the places were left desolate. And thus the face of the whole earth became deformed, because of the tempests, and the thunderings, and the lightnings, and the quaking of the earth.

And it came to pass that there was a thick darkness upon all the face of the land, insomuch that the inhabitants thereof who had not fallen could feel the vapor of darkness;

And there could be no light, because of the darkness, neither candles, neither torches, neither could there be fire kindled with their fine and exceedingly dry wood, so that there could not be any light at all;

And there was not any light sent, neither fire, neither the sun, nor the moon, nor the stars, for so great were the mists of darkness which were upon the face of the land.

And it came to pass that it did last for the space of three days and there was no light seen; and there was great mourning and howling and weeping among all the people continually; yea, great were the groanings of the people, because of the darkness and the great destruction which had come upon them.

3 Nephi 8:12–14, 17, 20–23

While the testimony above related to Mexico and Central America, the following could well have been at the same time, describing events primarily in Nevada, Utah and Arizona.

Washoe Indian Legend

Typical of these traditions is the following Washoe Indian legend, which seems to have preserved the story of the disappearance of the great intermountain lake. This immense "sheet" of water was called Lahonitan. Its existence in the past is attested to by the fossilized remains of animals that have been found in various parts of the basin, as well as by other unmistakable evidence. The Indian legend is related as follows:

Long time, heap long time. Maybe one hundred years, injun no sabe, white mane sabe. My grandfather's father, he heap old man. Maybe two, three hundreds years, me dunno, Carson Valley, Wasu Valley, Truckee Valley, Long Valley, Pilamid Lake, Lublockm eblywhere all water, plenty pish, plenty duck. Big pish too, now no see him no more, all go away, no come back.

Wasu Injun, he lib big mountains [pointing to the Comstock and Pyramid range]. Some time Wasu Indian take 'em boat go see Piutee, maybe Piutee he take 'em boat go see Wasu Indian. Yash he good friend, all time.

[Pointing to the Sierra to the west of Washoe Valley, the old Indian continued:]

Big mountain all time pire, plenty boom, boom, heap smoke, injun heap flaid! Byme bye, one day, mountain heap smoke, heap noise, glound too much shake, injund heap flaid, pall down, plenty cly. E sun ebly day come up (pointing to the northeast) he go down (pointing to the southwest). One day sun no come up, Injun no sabe, mountain heap smoke, glound pleny shake, wind blow, water heap mad. Maybe two, tlee day sun he no come, injun no eat, no sleep, all time cly, cly, yash, heap flaid. Byme bye water make plenty noise, go plenty fast like Tlukee Liver; water go down, down, mountain come up, come up, plenty mud, plenty pish die, byme, be sun come back over this mountain (pointing to the southeast) he go down ober there (pointing to the north-west). Yash, whiteman sabe, injun no sabe.

Maybe two, tlee week, mud he dly up, Piutee, Wasu Injun walk, no more boat. All water he go; maybe little water Pilamid Lake, Hone Lake, Wasu Lake, too much mountain, he come purty quick. Yash, injun no sabe water, big pish no come back. No see him more.

Mrs. M.M. Garwood, *Progressive West Magazine,* reprinted in *Deseret Semi-Weekly News,* February 5, 1906

The narrative is lacking in detail, but it is sufficiently clear to indicate that the Indians of early America have preserved, in legendary form, some account of the terrible cataclysms that have convulsed the American continents.

We would not be concerned if Darwin's evolutionary theory religionists did not force their blind faith and dogma on us and try to require our children to understand their single "one size fits all" theory. Teachers who are public servants supported by parents' taxes should be required, in fairness, to present creationists theories as an alternative explanation for life and the changes we see on the earth's surface. Why should one discredited theory be forced on everyone at tax-paying parental expense?

Recent geological surveys have discovered two major intelligently guided asteroid strikes that could well explain the Washoe Indian legend listed above to match the massive upheavals recorded by the witness of II Nephi preceding it.

The first asteroid strike discovered created a 100-mile implosion crater on the edge (20%) of the Yucatan Peninsula with the balance in the Gulf of Mexico.

The second strike was by an asteroid leaving an even larger 120-mile diameter implosion crater between Beatty, Nevada, and Cedar City, Utah.

The end results are easily explained and understood. Creationists stand in support of an intelligent anthropomorphic Father God who requires obedience before offering rewards. Also, they believe that

God will require a final judgment and eternal disposition of all mankind—the obedient to success and happiness, the disobedient, who are in "denial" relative to their creator's existence, to misery and pain.

The worst danger of Darwin's theory to young minds is that the youth decide that they are but highly-evolved animals, with no need to heed and obey their heaven-provided conscience. This in turn causes them to live carnal, sensual and devilish lives in the law of the jungle much to their sorrow and Satan's satisfaction. This is why parents who love their children cannot accept control of their children's minds by the NEA, the ACLU and Federal Aid to Education. The U.S. Constitution provides no Federal educational authority except that reserved to states' powers' clause of the Tenth Amendment. Both theories of origin must be taught either by private schools or by 1–12 schools returned to total parent, county funding and control. Educational administrators can resolve fairness problems. State and federal courts should not be permitted to hear such petty non-criminal problems. School teachers need to have uniform discipline, order and control if teaching and true education is to take place. The educational "censorship" of concepts opposed to a theory should be ended by a fair hearing of both concepts for every grade school child, and parental desires should carry the most weight. After all parents pay those tax-paid servants and are those held responsible by God to properly rear and educate their children. Why is it impossible to censor foul four-letter words and at the same time hypocritically censor the healthy concept that men are the children of god? Whatever entices men to pray is of God. But whatever entices not to pray is of Satan. The theory of evolution was not framed in heaven.

Our evolutionist "one theory fits all" folks have been unwilling to explore alternative concepts. This is especially onerous when it comes to interpretation of the meaning of several facts engraved in stone. In the book of *Mysteries of the Unexplained* published by *Reader's Digest* in 1982 and 1985, on pages 34 to 54 there is a chapter titled "Anomalies" which the scientific world appears to be actively trying to ignore our of existence. In this day of knowledge explosions and rapid communications that approach won't work.

"That dog has ceased to hunt." Records in rock make current biological evolutionary dogma ridiculous. Some of the things that must eventually be addressed by honest open minds are as follows:

In the *Reader's Digest* book *Mysteries of the Unexplained,* several photos show human footprints in stone alongside dinosaur tracks and the footprints of other animals and birds such as the turkey. A human sandal pressing a trilobite under its prints proves that either trilobites existed much longer than their theoretical extinction 280 million years ago, or that man lived on this earth at the same time. Shame on the University of Utah geologists, so tied to evolutionary incorrect principles that they, when the evidence was brought to them, refused to look at the rock-born sandal track pushing down a trilobite brought from Delta, Utah to the University of Utah.

On pages 126–128 of *Strange Stories of Alaska and the Yukon is* an opportunity for truth-seeking scholars to reassess several things.

The story tells of finding a petrified tree covered with 100 feet of dirt. The fact that it clearly shows ax chipping marks is cause to recognize that humans lived contemporary with the tree. This in turn puts a constant time requirement for tree petrifaction under a great deal of scrutiny. Aside from discussing the finding of mastodons frozen in the ice of Alaska and Siberia, the last section of the book, pages 133 to 153, gives some rather credible stories of mastodons still roaming Alaska contemporary with the 1890's gold rush.

The current brainwashed mindset refuses to admit that scripture is our only primary source of first-hand information extending before about 750 years B.C. Giant human footprints have been found from coast to coast in the U.S.A. No one has bothered to point out that in Genesis 6:4 they are mentioned before the baptism of the earth in the universal flood and also in Numbers 13:33. Are the "so-called scientists" interested in truths or are they afraid to give credence to scripture and God its originator? Are they fearful that too much light and evidence will bring their sacred grail—the monolithic use of the concept theory of evolution—crashing to earth like a heathen idol destroyed by an angry God? One thing is common in the scholastic world, to which men turn to as discoverer and protector of truths, is that their leading lights refuse to admit that there is much in every field that is not known. They, therefore, push beyond and often against clear evidence and cover all with the singular elastic theory of biological evolution. What each person seeking truth needs is a large "I don't know basket" into which unresolved concepts are placed until more light is available. There are many things that we will not resolve in one or two generations or in an average lifetime (even during this knowledge explosion). To have the honesty and patience to leave them in abeyance is difficult. However, if we are willing to do so, we can with clear open minds revisit and change old and outdated inadequate theories, replacing them with new theories until all the evidence is in and the theory is replaced by a true understanding. Trying to ignore challenging new data is similar to a snail following the top of a railroad track rail assuming that they won't get smashed, or like the Dutch boy forever holding back the flood with his thumb.

One of the most difficult things for those educated to a scholastic mindset is to view honestly the miracles of the Old and New Testaments. Those educated beyond their intelligence either attack scriptural miracles as fanciful fairy tales or attempt to ignore them. Unfortunately, they try to ignore all as being myth versus sound first witness historical reality. God's miracles operate on natural laws, often not yet understandable by men.

A more fair-minded method is to recognize that there are many things that happen that operate on natural laws we as yet do not understand nor comprehend. This is what is meant by the word miracle. Many modern editions of scripture expunge, downplay or twist the miraculous into a form they feel is understandable. The King James' Version of the Bible maintains the miraculous accounts for us to ponder and maintains the godship and the resurrection of Jesus instead of relegating him to the category of a prophet or great teacher. This is one of the reasons the King James' Version is the safest version. Often the more men interpret, the further they are from the truth.

When those in "scientific pursuits" become open-minded enough to study, like Einstein, *Earth in Upheaval* by Velikovsky, they will gain an understanding of what has happened on this earth in the past 13,000 years. There will no longer be significant resistance to schoolchildren learning of alternative theories. The current educational monopoly and censorship should and will pass as a discarded garment so that upcoming generations can follow the paths of truth, wherever the evidence leads, without control and free of the immoral and improper coercion by governmental power.

In conclusion, we find not only Egyptologists and scholastics resisting fresh concepts of the origin of man, but many theologians resisting change to traditional views. Recently, a wellread scriptorian said: "I am frightened by people who interpret the Bible literally." After reflection, that idea was rebuked by the statement, "I am not only frightened, but horrified by those that choose to turn any scriptural record into myth or allegory so it can match their faulty education." May we all search for truth and keep a large "I don't know basket" while disagreeing agreeably to promote the open-mindedness of oncoming generations in their search for truth. Remember that "Christian evolutionists" get the Lamb and the Lion to lay down together by permitting the Lion to eat the Lamb.

Velikovsky's book, *Earth in Upheaval*, literally rips the theory of evolution to shreds. He was the first to recognize the flaws in the early worship of carbon dating, which he discusses in *Earth in Upheaval*. His criticisms have caused a revision of the concepts of carbon dating. It is still useful but not accurate. The only accurate measure we have of the past is "tree ring science".

Scholars scoffed in the mid-1940s when *Worlds in Collision* was first published. Everyone was brainwashed to believe a silly illogical concept that the earth's petroleum deposits were created by dead dinosaurs.

Velikovsky told us that the rings around Venus were heavily laden with naphtha, which was thrown to earth during the near-pass of Venus. Venus looked like a bull and it is easy to accept that the Minotaur of Crete and the Baal or Bull worship of the near east and India stem from what was visible in the night skies in about 1573 B.C. The scientific world scoffed at and repressed Velikovsky's research. However, when the Venus probe went out thirty years later the rings were proven to be laden with naphtha. Velikovsky's supporters had the last laugh as usual. Searchers for understanding and for alternate explanations of unusual phenomena are invited and encouraged to go through inter-library loan to obtain the works of Velikovsky so they can read the evidence proven in his research and decide for themselves.

Some readers may have wondered why references in Section I and II are limited primarily to scripture. Nearly every theory in this work enjoys superior documentation within the writings of Immanuel Velikovsky to whom the author is greatly indebted and by whom he has been inspired to write these alternative theories with a bold hand.

CONCLUSION

The Evolutionist religious movement has held American "scientific" education as a captive monopoly since the Scopes Monkey Trial. Parents who pay the salaries should work to overthrow such blatant improper censorship and control of their children's minds and education.

The question is an intelligently guided creation vs. the luck of blind chance hidden behind the smokescreen of billions and billions of years.

Every child should have an honest presentation of the creation by an anthropomorphic father creator and, I suppose for the near term, a competing evolutionary by-chance explanation.

Not only should schools offer open-minded "science" courses, but schools and homes should also return to a serious study of the Scriptures and a recognition that the clues to the condition of the world they live in are abundant in scripture. Just as an auto mechanic uses an operations and repair manual, every soul needs to know that the scriptures are God's operation and repair manual. If we wish to live a happier life, in a better world, it is necessary for families to study and discuss all scripture and recognize it as the only pre-750 B.C. history we have written by man as it happened.

When the "scholastic" and "scientific" worlds are honest enough to analyze each of the events of the Bible that question the theory of evolution our society will return to the growth in knowledge under sound principles.

BONUS APPENDIX = U.S. CONSTITUTION

This document, in the purity of its original intent, will guide the Government of the whole world throughout the thousand years of the millennium when Christ returns to give the "Law from Zion" and the words of his Gospel from Jerusalem surrounded and supported by His original twelve Apostles.

IN CONGRESS, July 4, 1776

The unanimous Declaration of the thirteen United States of *America,*

When in the Course of human events, it becomes necessary for one people to dissolve the political bands which have connected them with another, and to assume among the powers of the earth, the separate and equal station to which the Laws of Nature and of Nature's God entitle them, a decent respect to the opinions of mankind requires that they should declare the causes which impel them to the separation.

We hold these truths to be self-evident, that all men are created equal, that they are endowed by their Creator with certain unalienable Rights, that among these are Life, Liberty and the pursuit of Happiness. That to secure these rights, Governments are instituted among Men, deriving their just powers from the consent of the governed. That whenever any Form of Government becomes destructive of these ends, it is the Right of the People to alter or to abolish it, and to institute new Government, laying its foundation on such principles and organizing its powers in such form, as to them shall seem most likely to effect their Safety and Happiness. Prudence, indeed, will dictate that Governments long established should not be changed for light and transient causes; and accordingly all experience hath shewn, that mankind are more disposed to suffer, while evils are sufferable, than to right themselves by abolishing the forms to which they are accustomed. But when a long train of abuses and usurpations, pursuing invariably the same Object evinces a design to reduce them under absolute Despotism, it is their right, it is their duty, to throw off such Government, and to provide new Guards for their future security. Such has been the patient sufferance of these Colonies; and such is now the necessity which constrains them to alter their former Systems of Government. The history of the present King of Great Britain is a history of repeated injuries and usurpations, all having in direct object the establishment of an absolute Tyranny over these States. To prove this, let Facts be submitted to a candid world.

He has refused his Assent to Laws, the most wholesome and necessary for the public good.

He has forbidden his Governors to pass Laws of immediate and pressing importance, unless suspended in their operation till his Assent should be obtained; and when so suspended, he has utterly neglected to attend to them.

He has refused to pass other Laws for the accommodation of large districts of people, unless those people would relinquish the right of Representation in the Legislature, a right inestimable to them and formidable to tyrants only.

He has called together legislative bodies at places unusual, uncomfortable, and distant from the depository of their public Records, for the sole purpose of fatiguing them into compliance with his measures.

He has dissolved Representative Houses repeatedly, for opposing with manly firmness his invasions on the rights of the people.

He has refused for a long time, after such dissolutions, to cause others to be elected; whereby the Legislative powers, incapable of Annihilation, have returned to the People at large for their exercise; the State remaining in the mean time exposed to all the dangers of invasion from without, and convulsions within.

He has endeavored to prevent the population of these States; for that purpose obstructing the Laws for Naturalization of Foreigners; refusing to pass others to encourage their migrations hither, and raising the conditions of new Appropriations of Lands.

He has obstructed the Administration of Justice, by refusing his

Assent to Laws for establishing Judiciary powers.

He has made Judges dependent on his Will alone, for the tenure of their offices, and the amount and payment of their salaries.

He has erected a multitude of New Offices, and sent hither swarms of Officers to harrass our people, and eat out their substance.

He has kept among us, in times of peace, Standing Armies without the Consent of our legislatures.

He has affected to render the Military independent of and superior to the Civil power.

He has combined with others to subject us to a jurisdiction foreign to our constitution, and unacknowledged by our laws; giving his Assent to their Acts of pretended Legislation:

For Quartering large bodies of armed troops among us:

For protecting them, by a mock Trial, from punishment for any Murders which they should commit on the Inhabitants of these States:

For cutting off our Trade with all parts of the world:

For imposing Taxes on us without our Consent:

For depriving us in many cases, of the benefits of Trial by Jury:

For transporting us beyond Seas to be tried for pretended offences

For abolishing the free System of English Laws in a neighbouring Province, establishing therein an Arbitrary government, and enlarging its Boundaries so as to render it at once an example and fit instrument for introducing the same absolute rule into these Colonies:

For taking away our Charters, abolishing our most valuable Laws, and altering fundamentally the Forms of our Governments:

For suspending our own Legislatures, and declaring themselves invested with power to legislate for us in all cases whatsoever.

He has abdicated Government here, by declaring us out of his Protection and waging War against us.

He has plundered our seas, ravaged our Coasts, burnt our towns, and destroyed the lives of our people.

He is at this time transporting large Armies of foreign Mercenaries to compleat the works of death, desolation and tyranny, already begun with circumstances of Cruelty & perfidy scarcely paralleled in the most barbarous ages, and totally unworthy the Head of a civilized nation.

He has constrained our fellow Citizens taken Captive on the high Seas to bear Arms against their Country, to become the executioners of their friends and Brethren, or to fall themselves by their Hands.

He has excited domestic insurrections amongst us, and has endeavoured to bring on the inhabitants of our frontiers, the merciless Indian Savages, whose known rule of warfare, is an undistinguished destruction of all ages, sexes and conditions.

In every stage of these Oppressions We have Petitioned for Redress in the most humble terms: Our repeated Petitions have been answered only by repeated injury. A Prince whose character is thus marked by every act which may define a Tyrant, is unfit to be the ruler of a free people.

Nor have We been wanting in attentions to our British brethren. We have warned them from time to time of attempts by their legislature to extend an unwarrantable jurisdiction over us. We have reminded them of the circumstances of our emigration and settlement here. We have appealed to their native justice and magnanimity, and we have conjured them by the ties of our common kindred to disavow these usurpations, which, would inevitably interrupt our connections and correspondence. They too have been deaf to the voice of justice and of consanguinity. We must, therefore, acquiesce in the necessity, which denounces our Separation, and hold them, as we hold the rest of mankind, Enemies in War, in Peace Friends.

We, therefore, the Representatives of the United States of America, in General Congress, Assembled, appealing to the Supreme Judge of the world for the rectitude of our intentions, do, in the Name, and by Authority of the good People of these Colonies, solemnly publish and declare, That these United Colonies are, and of Right ought to be Free and Independent States; that they are Absolved from all Allegiance to the British Crown, and that all political connection between them and the State of Great Britain, is and ought to be totally dissolved; and

that as Free and Independent States, they have full Power to levy War, conclude Peace, contract Alliances, establish Commerce, and to do all other Acts and Things which Independent States may of right do. And for the support of this Declaration, with a firm reliance on the protection of divine Providence, we mutually pledge to each other our Lives, our Fortunes and our sacred Honor.

The 56 signatures on the Declaration appear in the positions indicated:

[Column 1]
Georgia:
    Button Gwinnett
    Lyman Hall
    George Walton
[Column 2]
North Carolina:
    William Hooper
    Joseph Hewes
    John Penn
South Carolina:
    Edward Rutledge
    Thomas Heyward, Jr.
    Thomas Lynch, Jr.
    Arthur Middleton
[Column 3]
Massachusetts:
    John Hancock
Maryland:
    Samuel Chase
    William Paca
    Thomas Stone
    Charles Carroll of Carrollton
Virginia:
    George Wythe
    Richard Henry Lee
    Thomas Jefferson
    Benjamin Harrison

Thomas Nelson, Jr.
Francis Lightfoot Lee
Carter Braxton
[Column 4]
Pennsylvania:
    Robert Morris
    Benjamin Rush
    Benjamin Franklin
    John Morton
    George Clymer
    James Smith
    George Taylor
    James Wilson
    George Ross
Delaware:
    Caesar Rodney
    George Read
    Thomas McKean
[Column 5]
New York:
    William Floyd
    Philip Livingston
    Francis Lewis
    Lewis Morris
New Jersey:
    Richard Stockton
    John Witherspoon
    Francis Hopkinson

John Hart
Abraham Clark
[Column 6]
New Hampshire:
  Josiah Bartlett
  William Whipple
Massachusetts:
  Samuel Adams
  John Adams
  Robert Treat Paine
  Elbridge Gerry
Rhode Island:

Stephen Hopkins
William Ellery
Connecticut:
  Roger Sherman
  Samuel Huntington
  William Williams Oliver
    Wolcott
New Hampshire:
  Matthew Thornton

The Fate of the Fifty-six Men Who Signed the Declaration of Independence

Have you ever wondered what happened to the fifty-six men who signed the Declaration of Independence?

- Five signers were captured by the British as traitors and tortured before they died.
- Twelve had their homes ransacked and burned
- Two lost their sons serving in the Revolutionary Army, another had two sons captured.
- Nine of the fifty-six fought and died from wounds or hardships of the Revolutionary War.
- They signed and they pledged their lives, their fortunes and their sacred honor.

What kind of men were they?

Twenty-four were lawyers and jurists. Eleven were merchants, nine were farmers and large plantation owners; men of means, well educated. But they signed the Declaration of Independence knowing full well that the penalty would be death if they were captured.

Such were the stories and sacrifices of the American Revolution. These were not wild-eyed, rabble rousing ruffians. They were soft-spoken men of means and education. They had security, but they valued liberty more.

Standing tall, straight and unwavering, they pledged: "For the support of this declaration, with firm reliance on the protection of the divine providence, we mutually pledge to each other, our lives, our fortunes and our sacred honor."

They gave you and me a free and independent America. The history books never told you a lot about what happened in the Revolutionary War. We didn't just fight the British. we were British subjects at the time ahnd we fought our own government.

Some of us take these liberties so much for granted, but we shouldn't. So, take a few minutes while enjoying your 4th of July Holiday and silently thank these patriots. It's not much to ask for the price they paid. Remember: Freedom is never free!

Constitution of the United States of America

Note: The following text is a transcription of the Constitution in its original form. Items in hypertext have since been amended or superseded. The Signature Area of this transcription features hyperlinks to biographies of the delegates to the Constitutional Convention.

We the People of the United States, in Order to form a more perfect Union, establish Justice, insure domestic Tranquility, provide for the common defense, promote the general Welfare, and secure the Blessings of Liberty to ourselves and our Posterity, do ordain and establish this Constitution for the United States of America.

ARTICLE I

Section. 1.
All legislative Powers herein granted shall be vested in a Congress of the United States, which shall consist of a Senate and House of Representatives.

Section. 2.
The House of Representatives shall be composed of Members chosen every second Year by the People of the several States, and the Electors in each State shall have the Qualifications requisite for Electors of the most numerous Branch of the State Legislature.

No Person shall be a Representative who shall not have attained to the Age of twenty five Years, and been seven Years a Citizen of the United States, and who shall not, when elected, be an Inhabitant of that State in which he shall be chosen.

Representatives and direct Taxes shall be apportioned among the several States which may be included within this Union, according to their respective Numbers, which shall be determined by adding to the whole Number of free Persons, including those bound to Service for a Term of Years, and excluding Indians not taxed, three fifths of all other Persons. The actual Enumeration shall be made within three Years after the first Meeting of the Congress of the United States, and within every subsequent Term of ten Years, in such Manner as they shall by Law direct. The Number of Representatives shall not exceed one for every thirty Thousand, but each State shall have at Least one Representative; and until such enumeration shall be made, the State of New Hampshire shall be entitled to chuse three, Massachusetts eight, Rhode-Island and Providence Plantations one, Connecticut five, New-York six, New Jersey four, Pennsylvania eight, Delaware one, Maryland six, Virginia ten, North Carolina five, South Carolina five, and Georgia three.

When vacancies happen in the Representation from any State, the Executive Authority thereof shall issue Writs of Election to fill such Vacancies.

The House of Representatives shall chuse their Speaker and other Officers; and shall have the sole Power of Impeachment.

Section. 3

The Senate of the United States shall be composed of two Senators from each State, <u>chosen by the Legislature thereof</u> for six Years; and each Senator shall have one Vote.

Immediately after they shall be assembled in Consequence of the first Election, they shall be divided as equally as may be into three Classes. The Seats of the Senators of the first Class shall be vacated at the Expiration of the second Year, of the second Class at the Expiration of the fourth Year, and of the third Class at the Expiration of the sixth Year, so that one third may be chosen every second Year; <u>and if Vacancies happen by Resignation, or otherwise, during the Recess of the Legislature of any State, the</u> Executive <u>thereof may make temporary Appointments until the</u> next Meeting <u>of the Legislature, which shall then fill such</u> Vacancies.

No Person shall be a Senator who shall not have attained to the Age of thirty Years, and been nine Years a Citizen of the United States, and who shall not, when elected, be an Inhabitant of that State for which he shall be chosen.

The Vice President of the United States shall be President of the Senate, but shall have no Vote, unless they be equally divided.

The Senate shall chuse their other Officers, and also a President pro tempore, in the Absence of the Vice President, or when he shall exercise the Office of President of the United States.

The Senate shall have the sole Power to try all Impeachments. When sitting for that Purpose, they shall be on Oath or Affirmation. When the President of the United States is tried, the Chief Justice shall preside: And no Person shall be convicted without the Concurrence of two thirds of the Members present.

Judgment in Cases of Impeachment shall not extend further than to removal from Office, and disqualification to hold and enjoy any Office of honor, Trust or Profit under the United States: but the Party convicted shall nevertheless be liable and subject to Indictment, Trial, Judgment and Punishment, according to Law.

Section. 4.

The Times, Places and Manner of holding Elections for Senators and Representatives, shall be prescribed in each State by the Legislature thereof; but the Congress may at any time by Law make or alter such Regulations, except as to the Places of chusing Senators.

The Congress shall assemble at least once in every Year, and such Meeting shall <u>be on the first Monday in December,</u> unless they shall by Law appoint a different Day.

Section. 5.

Each House shall be the Judge of the Elections, Returns and Qualifications of its own Members, and a Majority of each shall constitute a Quorum to do Business; but a smaller Number may adjourn from day to day, and may be authorized to compel the Attendance of absent Members, in such Manner, and under such Penalties as each House may provide.

Each House may determine the Rules of its Proceedings, punish its Members for disorderly Behavior, and, with the Concurrence of two thirds, expel a Member.

Each House shall keep a Journal of its Proceedings, and from time to time publish the same, excepting such Parts as may in their Judgment require Secrecy; and the Yeas and Nays of the Members of either House on any question shall, at the Desire of one fifth of those Present, be entered on the Journal.

Neither House, during the Session of Congress, shall, without the Consent of the other, adjourn for more than three days, nor to any other Place than that in which the two Houses shall be sitting.

Section. 6

The Senators and Representatives shall receive a Compensation for their Services, to be ascertained by Law, and paid out of the Treasury of the United States. They shall in all Cases, except Treason, Felony and Breach of the Peace, be privileged from Arrest during their Attendance at the Session of their respective Houses, and in going to and returning from the same; and for any Speech or Debate in either House, they shall not be questioned in any other Place.

No Senator or Representative shall, during the Time for which he was elected, be appointed to any civil Office under the Authority of the United States, which shall have been created, or the Emoluments whereof shall have been increased during such time; and no Person holding any Office under the United States, shall be a Member of either House during his Continuance in Office.

Section. 7

All Bills for raising Revenue shall originate in the House of Representatives; but the Senate may propose or concur with Amendments as on other Bills.

Every Bill which shall have passed the House of Representatives and the Senate, shall, before it become a Law, be presented to the President of the United States: If he approve he shall sign it, but if not he shall return it, with his Objections to that House in which it shall have originated, who shall enter the Objections at large on their Journal, and proceed to reconsider it. If after such Reconsideration two thirds of that House shall agree to pass the Bill, it shall be sent, together with the Objections, to the other House, by which it shall likewise be reconsidered, and if approved by two thirds of that House, it shall become a Law. But in all such Cases the Votes of both Houses shall be determined by yeas and Nays, and the Names of the Persons voting for and against the Bill shall be entered on the Journal of each House respectively. If any Bill shall not be returned by the President within ten Days (Sundays excepted) after it shall have been presented to him, the Same shall be a Law, in like Manner as if he had signed it, unless the Congress by their Adjournment prevent its Return, in which Case it shall not be a Law.

Every Order, Resolution, or Vote to which the Concurrence of the Senate and House of Representatives may be necessary (except on a question of Adjournment) shall be presented to the President of the United States; and before the Same shall take Effect, shall be approved by him, or being disapproved by him, shall be repassed by two thirds of the Senate and House of Representatives, according to the Rules and Limitations prescribed in the Case of a Bill.

Section. 8

The Congress shall have Power To lay and collect Taxes, Duties, Imposts and Excises, to pay the Debts and provide for the common Defence and general Welfare of the United States; but all Duties, Imposts and Excises shall be uniform throughout the United States;

To borrow Money on the credit of the United States;

To regulate Commerce with foreign Nations, and among the several States, and with the Indian Tribes;

To establish an uniform Rule of Naturalization, and uniform Laws on the subject of Bankruptcies throughout the United States;

To coin Money, regulate the Value thereof, and of foreign Coin, and fix the Standard of Weights and Measures;

To provide for the Punishment of counterfeiting the Securities and current Coin of the United States;

To establish Post Offices and post Roads;

To promote the Progress of Science and useful Arts, by securing for limited Times to Authors and Inventors the exclusive Right to their respective Writings and Discoveries;

To constitute Tribunals inferior to the supreme Court;

To define and punish Piracies and Felonies committed on the high Seas, and Offences against the Law of Nations;

To declare War, grant Letters of Marque and Reprisal, and make Rules concerning Captures on Land and Water;

To raise and support Armies, but no Appropriation of Money to that Use shall be for a longer Term than two Years;

To provide and maintain a Navy;

To make Rules for the Government and Regulation of the land and naval Forces;

To provide for calling forth the Militia to execute the Laws of the Union, suppress Insurrections and repel Invasions;

To provide for organizing, arming, and disciplining, the Militia, and for governing such Part of them as may be employed in the Service of the United States, reserving to the States respectively, the Appointment of the Officers, and the Authority of training the Militia according to the discipline prescribed by Congress;

To exercise exclusive Legislation in all Cases whatsoever, over such District (not exceeding ten Miles square) as may, by Cession of particular States, and the Acceptance of Congress, become the Seat of the Government of the United States, and to exercise like Authority over all Places purchased by the Consent of the Legislature of the State in which the Same shall be, for the Erection of Forts, Magazines, Arsenals, dock-Yards, and other needful Buildings; And

To make all Laws which shall be necessary and proper for carrying into Execution the foregoing Powers, and all other Powers vested by this Constitution in the Government of the United States, or in any Department or Officer thereof.

Section. 9

The Migration or Importation of such Persons as any of the States now existing shall think proper to admit, shall not be prohibited by the Congress prior to the Year one thousand eight hundred and eight, but a Tax or duty may be imposed on such Importation, not exceeding ten dollars for each Person.

The Privilege of the Writ of Habeas Corpus shall not be suspended, unless when in Cases of Rebellion or Invasion the public Safety may require it.

No Bill of Attainder or ex post facto Law shall be passed.

No Capitation, or other direct, Tax shall be laid, unless in Proportion to the Census or enumeration herein before directed to be taken.

No Tax or Duty shall be laid on Articles exported from any State.

No Preference shall be given by any Regulation of Commerce or Revenue to the Ports of one State over those of another; nor shall Vessels bound to, or from, one State, be obliged to enter, clear, or pay Duties in another.

No Money shall be drawn from the Treasury, but in Consequence of Appropriations made by Law; and a regular Statement and Account of the Receipts and Expenditures of all public Money shall be published from time to time.

No Title of Nobility shall be granted by the United States: And no Person holding any Office of Profit or Trust under them, shall, without the Consent of the Congress, accept of any present, Emolument, Office, or Title, of any kind whatever, from any King, Prince, or foreign State.

Section. 10.

No State shall enter into any Treaty, Alliance, or Confederation; grant Letters of Marque and Reprisal; coin Money; emit Bills of Credit; make any Thing but gold and silver Coin a Tender in Payment of Debts; pass any Bill of Attainder, ex post facto Law, or Law impairing the Obligation of Contracts, or grant any Title of Nobility.

No State shall, without the Consent of the Congress, lay any Imposts or Duties on Imports or Exports, except what may be absolutely necessary for executing its inspection Laws: and the net Produce of all Duties and Imposts, laid by any State on Imports or Exports, shall be for the Use of the Treasury of the United States; and all such Laws shall be subject to the Revision and Controul of the Congress.

No State shall, without the Consent of Congress, lay any Duty of Tonnage, keep Troops, or Ships of War in time of Peace, enter into any Agreement or Compact with another State, or with a foreign Power, or engage in War, unless actually invaded, or in such imminent Danger as will not admit of delay.

ARTICLE II

Section. 1.
The executive Power shall be vested in a President of the United States of America. He shall hold his Office during the Term of four Years, and, together with the Vice President, chosen for the same Term, be elected, as follows:

Each State shall appoint, in such Manner as the Legislature thereof may direct, a Number of Electors, equal to the whole Number of Senators and Representatives to which the State may be entitled in the Congress: but no Senator or Representative, or Person holding an Office of Trust or Profit under the United States, shall be appointed an Elector.

The Electors shall meet in their respective States, and vote by Ballot for two Persons, of whom one at least shall not be an Inhabitant of the same State with themselves. And they shall make a List of all the Persons voted for, and of the Number of Votes for each; which List they shall sign and certify, and transmit sealed to the Seat of the Government of the United States, directed to the President of the Senate. The President of the Senate shall, in the Presence of the Senate and House of Representatives, open all the Certificates, and the Votes shall then be counted. The Person having the greatest Number of Votes shall be the President, if such Number be a Majority of the whole Number of Electors appointed; and if there be more than one who have such Majority, and have an equal Number of Votes, then the House of Representatives shall immediately chuse by Ballot one of them for President; and if no Person have a Majority, then from the five highest on the List the said House shall in like Manner chuse the President. But in chusing the President, the Votes shall be taken by States, the Representation from each State having one Vote; A quorum for this purpose shall consist of a Member or Members from two thirds of the States, and a Majority of all the States shall be necessary to a Choice. In every Case, after the Choice of the President, the Person having the greatest Number of Votes of the Electors shall be the Vice President. But if there should remain two or more who have equal Votes, the

Senate shall chuse from them by Ballot the Vice President.

The Congress may determine the Time of chusing the Electors, and the Day on which they shall give their Votes; which Day shall be the same throughout the United States.

No Person except a natural born Citizen, or a Citizen of the United States, at the time of the Adoption of this Constitution, shall be eligible to the Office of President; neither shall any Person be eligible to that Office who shall not have attained to the Age of thirty five Years, and been fourteen Years a Resident within the United States.

In Case of the Removal of the President from Office, or of his Death, Resignation, or Inability to discharge the Powers and Duties of the said Office, the Same shall devolve on the Vice President, and the Congress may by Law provide for the Case of Removal, Death, Resignation or Inability, both of the President and Vice President, declaring what Officer shall then act as President, and such Officer shall act accordingly, until the Disability be removed, or a President shall be elected.

The President shall, at stated Times, receive for his Services, a Compensation, which shall neither be increased nor diminished during the Period for which he shall have been elected, and he shall not receive within that Period any other Emolument from the United States, or any of them.

Before he enter on the Execution of his Office, he shall take the following Oath or Affirmation: "I do solemnly swear (or affirm) that I will faithfully execute the Office of President of the United States, and will to the best of my Ability, preserve, protect and defend the Constitution of the United States."

Section. 2
The President shall be Commander in Chief of the Army and Navy of the United States, and of the Militia of the several States, when called into the actual Service of the United States; he may require the Opinion, in writing, of the principal Officer in each of the executive Departments, upon any Subject relating to the Duties of their respective Offices, and he shall have Power to grant Reprieves and Pardons for Offences against the United States, except in Cases of

Impeachment.

He shall have Power, by and with the Advice and Consent of the Senate, to make Treaties, provided two thirds of the Senators present concur; and he shall nominate, and by and with the Advice and Consent of the Senate, shall appoint Ambassadors, other public Ministers and Consuls, Judges of the supreme Court, and all other Officers of the United States, whose Appointments are not herein otherwise provided for, and which shall be established by Law: but the Congress may by Law vest the Appointment of such inferior Officers, as they think proper, in the President alone, in the Courts of Law, or in the Heads of Departments.

The President shall have Power to fill up all Vacancies that may happen during the Recess of the Senate, by granting Commissions which shall expire at the End of their next Session.

Section. 3
He shall from time to time give to the Congress Information of the State of the Union, and recommend to their Consideration such Measures as he shall judge necessary and expedient; he may, on extraordinary Occasions, convene both Houses, or either of them, and in Case of Disagreement between them, with Respect to the Time of Adjournment, he may adjourn them to such Time as he shall think proper; he shall receive Ambassadors and other public Ministers; he shall take Care that the Laws be faithfully executed, and shall Commission all the Officers of the United States.

Section. 4
The President, Vice President and all civil Officers of the United States, shall be removed from Office on Impeachment for, and Conviction of, Treason, Bribery, or other high Crimes and Misdemeanors.

ARTICLE III

Section. 1
The judicial Power of the United States shall be vested in one supreme Court, and in such inferior Courts as the Congress may

from time to time ordain and establish. The Judges, both of the supreme and inferior Courts, shall hold their Offices during good Behaviour, and shall, at stated Times, receive for their Services a Compensation, which shall not be diminished during their Continuance in Office.

Section. 2

The judicial Power shall extend to all Cases, in Law and Equity, arising under this Constitution, the Laws of the United States, and Treaties made, or which shall be made, under their Authority; to all Cases affecting Ambassadors, other public Ministers and Consuls; to all Cases of admiralty and maritime Jurisdiction; to Controversies to which the United States shall be a Party; to Controversies between two or more States; between a State and Citizens of another State; between Citizens of different States; between Citizens of the same State claiming Lands under Grants of different States, and between a State, or the Citizens thereof, and foreign States, Citizens or Subjects.

In all Cases affecting Ambassadors, other public Ministers and Consuls, and those in which a State shall be Party, the supreme Court shall have original Jurisdiction. In all the other Cases before mentioned, the supreme Court shall have appellate Jurisdiction, both as to Law and Fact, with such Exceptions, and under such Regulations as the Congress shall make.

The Trial of all Crimes, except in Cases of Impeachment, shall be by Jury; and such Trial shall be held in the State where the said Crimes shall have been committed; but when not committed within any State, the Trial shall be at such Place or Places as the Congress may by Law have directed.

Section. 3

Treason against the United States, shall consist only in levying War against them, or in adhering to their Enemies, giving them Aid and Comfort. No Person shall be convicted of Treason unless on the Testimony of two Witnesses to the same overt Act, or on Confession in open Court.

The Congress shall have Power to declare the Punishment of

Treason, but no Attainder of Treason shall work Corruption of Blood, or Forfeiture except during the Life of the Person attainted.

ARTICLE IV

Section. 1
Full Faith and Credit shall be given in each State to the public Acts, Records, and judicial Proceedings of every other State. And the Congress may by general Laws prescribe the Manner in which such Acts, Records and Proceedings shall be proved, and the Effect thereof.

Section. 2
The Citizens of each State shall be entitled to all Privileges and Immunities of Citizens in the several States.

A Person charged in any State with Treason, Felony, or other Crime, who shall flee from Justice, and be found in another State, shall on Demand of the executive Authority of the State from which he fled, be delivered up, to be removed to the State having Jurisdiction of the Crime.

No Person held to Service or Labour in one State, under the Laws thereof, escaping into another, shall, in Consequence of any Law or Regulation therein, be discharged from such Service or Labour, but shall be delivered up on Claim of the Party to whom such Service or Labour may be due.

Section 3
New States may be admitted by the Congress into this Union; but no new State shall be formed or erected within the Jurisdiction of any other State; nor any State be formed by the Junction of two or more States, or Parts of States, without the Consent of the Legislatures of the States concerned as well as of the Congress.

The Congress shall have Power to dispose of and make all needful Rules and Regulations respecting the Territory or other Property belonging to the United States; and nothing in this Constitution shall be so construed as to Prejudice any Claims of the United States, or of any particular State.

Section 4
The United States shall guarantee to every State in this Union a Republican Form of Government, and shall protect each of them against Invasion; and on Application of the Legislature, or of the Executive (when the Legislature cannot be convened), against domestic Violence.

ARTICLE V

The Congress, whenever two thirds of both Houses shall deem it necessary, shall propose Amendments to this Constitution, or, on the Application of the Legislatures of two thirds of the several States, shall call a Convention for proposing Amendments, which,in either Case, shall be valid to all Intents and Purposes, as Part of this Constitution, when ratified by the Legislatures of three fourths of the several States, or by Conventions in three fourths thereof, as the one or the other Mode of Ratification may be proposed by the Congress; Provided that no Amendment which may be made prior to the Year One thousand eight hundred and eight shall in any Manner affect the first and fourth Clauses in the Ninth Section of the first Article; and that no State, without its Consent, shall be deprived of its equal Suffrage in the Senate.

ARTICLE VI

All Debts contracted and Engagements entered into, before the Adoption of this Constitution, shall be as valid against the United States under this Constitution, as under the Confederation.

This Constitution, and the Laws of the United States which shall be made in Pursuance thereof; and all Treaties made, or which shall be made, under the Authority of the United States, shall be the supreme Law of the Land; and the Judges in every State shall be bound thereby, any Thing in the Constitution or Laws of any State to the Contrary notwithstanding.

The Senators and Representatives before mentioned, and the Members of the several State Legislatures, and all executive and judicial Officers, both of the United States and of the several States, shall be bound by Oath or Affirmation, to support this Constitution; but no religious Test shall ever be required as a Qualification to any

Office or public Trust under the United States.

ARTICLE VII

The Ratification of the Conventions of nine States, shall be sufficient for the Establishment of this Constitution between the States
so ratifying the Same.

The Word, "the," being interlined between the seventh and
eighth Lines of the first Page, the Word "Thirty" being partly written on an Erazure in the fifteenth Line of the first Page, The Words
"is tried" being interlined between the thirty second and thirty third
Lines of the first Page and the Word "the" being interlined between
the forty third and forty fourth Lines of the second Page.

Attest William Jackson Secretary

Done in Convention by the Unanimous Consent of the States
present the Seventeenth Day of September in the Year of our
Lord one thousand seven hundred and Eighty seven and of the
Independence of the United States of America the Twelfth In
witness whereof We have hereunto subscribed our Names, G$^\circ$.
Washington

In Convention Monday September 17th. 1787
Present
The States of

New Hampshire, Massachusetts, Connecticut, Mr. Hamilton from
New York, New Jersey, Pennsylvania, Delaware, Maryland,
Virginia, North Carolina, South Carolina and Georgia.

Resolved,

That the preceding Constitution be laid before the United States in
Congress assembled, and that it is the Opinion of this Convention,
that it should afterwards be submitted to a Convention of Delegates,
chosen in each State by the People thereof, under the Recom-
mendation of its Legislature, for their Assent and Ratification; and
that each Convention assenting to, and ratifying the Same, should
give Notice thereof to the United States in Congress assembled.

Resolved, That it is the Opinion of this Convention, that as soon as the Conventions of nine States shall have ratified this Constitution, the United States in Congress assembled should fix a Day on which Electors should be appointed by the States which shall have ratified the same, and a Day on which the Electors should assemble to vote for the President, and the Time and place for commencing Proceedings under this Constitution. That after such Publication the Electors should be appointed, and the Senators and Representatives elected: That the Electors should meet on the Day fixed for the Election of the President, and should transmit their votes certified signed, sealed and directed, as the Constitution requires, to the Secretary of the United States in Congress assembled, that the Senators and Representatives should convene at the Time and Place assigned; that the Senators should appoint a President of the Senate, for the sole Purpose of receiving, opening and counting the Votes for President; and, that after he shall be chosen, the Congress, together with the President, should, without Delay, proceed to execute this Constitution.

By the Unanimous Order of the Convention
Go: Washington President.
W. Jackson Secretary

The BILL OF RIGHTS
As provided in the FIRST TEN AMENDMENTS TO THE
CONTITUTION OF THE UNITED STATES Effective December
15, 1791

Articles in addition to, and Amendment of the Constitution of the United States of America, proposed by Congress, and ratified by the Legislatures of the several States, pursuant to the fifth Article of the original Constitution.

THE PREAMBLE TO THE BILL OF RIGHTS
Congress of the United States
begun and held at the City of New-York, on
Wednesday the fourth of March, one thousand seven hundred
and eighty nine.

THE Conventions of a number of the States, having at the time of their adopting the Constitution, expressed a desire, in order to prevent misconstruction or abuse of its powers, that further declaratory and restrictive clauses should be added: And as extending the ground of public confidence in the Government, will best ensure the beneficent ends of its institution.

RESOLVED by the Senate and House of Representatives of the United States of America, in Congress assembled, two thirds of both Houses concurring, that the following Articles be proposed to the Legislatures of the several States, as amendments to the Constitution of the United States, all, or any of which Articles, when ratified by three fourths of the said Legislatures, to be valid to all intents and purposes, as part of the said Constitution; viz.

ARTICLES in addition to, and Amendment of the Constitution of the United States of America, proposed by Congress, and ratified by the Legislatures of the several States, pursuant to the fifth Article of the original Constitution.

THE FIRST 10 AMENDMENTS TO THE CONSTITUTION AS RATIFIED BY THE STATES
Note: The following text is a transcription of the first 10 amendments to the Constitution in their original form. These amendments were ratified December 15, 1791, and form what is known as the "Bill of Rights."

Amendment I

Congress shall make no law respecting an establishment of religion, or prohibiting the free exercise thereof; or abridging the freedom of speech, or of the press; or the right of the people peaceably to assemble, and to petition the Government for a redress of grievances.

Amendment II

A well regulated Militia, being necessary to the security of a free State, the right of the people to keep and bear Arms, shall not be infringed.

Amendment III

No Soldier shall, in time of peace be quartered in any house, without the consent of the Owner, nor in time of war, but in a manner to be prescribed by law.

Amendment IV

The right of the people to be secure in their persons, houses, papers, and effects, against unreasonable searches and seizures, shall not be violated, and no Warrants shall issue, but upon probable cause, supported by Oath or affirmation, and particularly describing the place to be searched, and the persons or things to be seized.

Amendment V

No person shall be held to answer for a capital, or otherwise infamous crime, unless on a presentment or indictment of a Grand Jury, except in cases arising in the land or naval forces, or in the Militia, when in actual service in time of War or public danger; nor shall any person be subject for the same offence to be twice put in jeopardy of life or limb; nor shall be compelled in any criminal case to be a witness against himself, nor be deprived of life, liberty, or property, without due process of law; nor shall private property be taken for public use, without just compensation.

Amendment VI

In all criminal prosecutions, the accused shall enjoy the right to a speedy and public trial, by an impartial jury of the State and district wherein the crime shall have been committed, which district shall have been previously ascertained by law, and to be informed of the nature and cause of the accusation; to be confronted with the witnesses against him; to have compulsory process for obtaining witnesses in his favor, and to have the Assistance of Counsel for his defence.

Amendment VII

In suits at common law, where the value in controversy shall exceed twenty dollars, the right of trial by jury shall be preserved, and no fact tried by a jury, shall be otherwise reexamined in any Court of the United States, than according to the rules of the common law.

Amendment VIII

Excessive bail shall not be required, nor excessive fines imposed, nor cruel and unusual punishments inflicted.

Amendment IX

The enumeration in the Constitution, of certain rights, shall not be construed to deny or disparage others retained by the people.

Amendment X

The powers not delegated to the United States by the Constitution, nor prohibited by it to the States, are reserved to the States respectively, or to the people.

Amendment XI

Passed by Congress March 4, 1794. Ratified February 7, 1795.

Note: Article III, section 2, of the Constitution was modified by amendment 11.

The Judicial power of the United States shall not be construed to extend to any suit in law or equity, commenced or prosecuted against one of the United States by Citizens of another State, or by Citizens or Subjects of any Foreign State.

Amendment XII

Passed by Congress December 9, 1803. Ratified June 15, 1804.

NOTE: A portion of Article II, section 1 of the Constitution was superseded by the 12th amendment.

The Electors shall meet in their respective states and vote by ballot for President and Vice-President, one of whom, at least, shall not be an inhabitant of the same state with themselves; they shall name in their ballots the person voted for as President, and in distinct ballots the person voted for as Vice-President, and they shall make distinct lists of all persons voted for as President, and of all persons voted for as Vice-President, and of the number ofvotes for each, which lists they shall sign and certify, and transmit sealed to the seat of the government of the United States, directed to the President of the Senate; the President of the Senate shall, in the presence of the Senate and House of Representatives, open all the certificates and the votes shall then be counted; The person having the greatest number of votes for President, shall be the President, if such number be a majority of the whole number of Electors appointed; and if no person have such majority, then from the persons having the highest numbers not exceeding three on the list of those voted for as President, the House of Representatives shall choose immediately, by ballot, the President. But in choosing the President, the votes shall be taken by states, the representation from each state having one vote; a quorum for this purpose shall consist of a member or members from two-thirds of the states, and a majority of all the states shall be necessary to a choice. [And if the House of

Representatives shall not choose a President whenever the right of choice shall devolve upon them, before the fourth day of March next following, then the Vice-President shall act as President, as in case of the death or other constitutional disability of the President.]* The person having the greatest number of votes as Vice-President, shall be the Vice-President, if such number be a majority of the whole number of Electors appointed, and if no person have a majority, then from the two highest numbers on the list, the Senate shall choose the Vice-President; a quorum for the purpose shall consist of two thirds of the whole number of Senators, and a majority of the whole number shall be necessary to a choice. But no person constitutionally ineligible to the office of President shall be eligible to that of Vice-President of the United States.

Superseded by section 3 of the 20th amendment.

Amendment XIII

Passed by Congress January 31, 1865. Ratified December 6, 1865.

Note: A portion of Article IV, section 2, of the Constitution was superseded by the 13th amendment.

Section 1
Neither slavery nor involuntary servitude, except as a punishment for crime whereof the party shall have been duly convicted, shall exist within the United States, or any place subject to their jurisdiction.

Section 2
Congress shall have power to enforce this article by appropriate legislation.

Amendment XIV

Passed by Congress June 13, 1866. Ratified July 9, 1868.

Note: Article I, section 2, of the Constitution was modified by section 2 of the 14th amendment.

Section 1

All persons born or naturalized in the United States, and subject to the jurisdiction thereof, are citizens of the United States and of the State wherein they reside. No State shall make or enforce any law which shall abridge the privileges or immunities of citizens of the United States; nor shall any State deprive any person of life, liberty, or property, without due process of law; nor deny to any person within its jurisdiction the equal protection of the laws.

Section 2

Representatives shall be apportioned among the several States according to their respective numbers, counting the whole number of persons in each State, excluding Indians not taxed. But when the right to vote at any election for the choice of electors for President and Vice-President of the United States, Representatives in Congress, the Executive and Judicial officers of a State, or the members of the Legislature thereof, is denied to any of the male inhabitants of such State, being twenty-one years of age,* and citizens of the United States, or in any way abridged, except for participation in rebellion, or other crime, the basis of representation therein shall be reduced in the proportion which the number of such male citizens shall bear to the whole number of male citizens twenty-one years of age in such State.

Section 3

No person shall be a Senator or Representative in Congress, or elector of President and Vice-President, or hold any office, civil or military, under the United States, or under any State, who, having previously taken an oath, as a member of Congress, or as an officer of the United States, or as a member of any State legislature, or as an executive or judicial officer of any State, to support the Constitution of the United States, shall have engaged in insurrection or rebellion against the same, or given aid or comfort to the enemies thereof. But Congress may by a vote of two-thirds of each House, remove such disability.

Section 4
The validity of the public debt of the United States, authorized by law, including debts incurred for payment of pensions and bounties for services in suppressing insurrection or rebellion, shall not be questioned. But neither the United States nor any State shall assume or pay any debt or obligation incurred in aid of insurrection or rebellion against the United States, or any claim for the loss or emancipation of any slave; but all such debts, obligations and claims shall be held illegal and void.

Section 5
The Congress shall have the power to enforce, by appropriate legislation, the provisions of this article. *Changed by section 1 of the 26th amendment.*

Amendment XV

Passed by Congress February 26, 1869. Ratified February 3, 1870.

Section 1
The right of citizens of the United States to vote shall not be denied or abridged by the United States or by any State on account of race, color, or previous condition of servitude.

Section 2
The Congress shall have the power to enforce this article by appropriate legislation.
Note: Most of the Amendments of the twentieth century i.e. XVI through XXVII appear to have weakened the American Republic. They should come under scrutiny for repeal or revision.

Amendment XVI

Passed by Congress July 2, 1909. Ratified February 3, 1913.

Note: Article I, section 9, of the Constitution was modified by amendment 16.

The Congress shall have power to lay and collect taxes on incomes, from whatever source derived, without apportionment among the several States, and without regard to any census or enumeration.

Amendment XVII

Passed by Congress May 13, 1912. Ratified April 8, 1913.

Note: Article I, section 3, of the Constitution was modified by the 17th amendment.

The Senate of the United States shall be composed of two Senators from each State, elected by the people thereof, for six years; and each Senator shall have one vote. The electors in each State shall have the qualifications requisite for electors of the most numerous branch of the State legislatures.

When vacancies happen in the representation of any State in the Senate, the executive authority of such State shall issue writs of election to fill such vacancies: *Provided,* That the legislature of any State may empower the executive thereof to make temporary appointments until the people fill the vacancies by election as the legislature may direct.

This amendment shall not be so construed as to affect the election or term of any Senator chosen before it becomes valid as part of the Constitution.

Amendment XVIII

Passed by Congress December 18, 1917. Ratified January 16, 1919. Repealed by amendment 21.

Section 1
After one year from the ratification of this article the manufacture, sale, or transportation of intoxicating liquors within, the importation thereof into, or the exportation thereof from the United States and all territory subject to the jurisdiction thereof for beverage purposes is hereby prohibited.

Section 2
The Congress and the several States shall have concurrent power to enforce this article by appropriate legislation.

Section 3
This article shall be inoperative unless it shall have been ratified as an amendment to the Constitution by the legislatures of the several States, as provided in the Constitution, within seven years from the date of the submission hereof to the States by the Congress.

Amendment XIX

Passed by Congress June 4, 1919. Ratified August 18, 1920.

The right of citizens of the United States to vote shall not be denied or abridged by the United States or by any State on account of sex.
    Congress shall have power to enforce this article by appropriate legislation.

Amendment XX

Passed by Congress March 2, 1932. Ratified January 23, 1933.

Note: Article I, section 4, of the Constitution was modified by section 2 of this amendment. In addition, a portion of the 12th amendment was superseded by section 3.

Section 1
The terms of the President and the Vice President shall end at noon on the 20th day of January, and the terms of Senators and Representatives at noon on the 3d day of January, of the years in which such terms would have ended if this article had not been ratified; and the terms of their successors shall then begin.

Section 2
The Congress shall assemble at least once in every year, and such meeting shall begin at noon on the 3d day of January, unless they

shall by law appoint a different day.

Section 3

If, at the time fixed for the beginning of the term of the President, the President elect shall have died, the Vice President elect shall become President. If a President shall not have been chosen before the time fixed for the beginning of his term, or if the President elect shall have failed to qualify, then the Vice President elect shall act as President until a President shall have qualified; and the Congress may by law provide for the case wherein neither a President elect nor a Vice President shall have qualified, declaring who shall then act as President, or the manner in which one who is to act shall be selected, and such person shall act accordingly until a President or Vice President shall have qualified.

Section 4

The Congress may by law provide for the case of the death of any of the persons from whom the House of Representatives may choose a President whenever the right of choice shall have devolved upon them, and for the case of the death of any of the persons from whom the Senate may choose a Vice President whenever the right of choice shall have devolved upon them.

Section 5

Sections 1 and 2 shall take effect on the 15th day of October following the ratification of this article.

Section 6

This article shall be inoperative unless it shall have been ratified as an amendment to the Constitution by the legislatures of three fourths of the several States within seven years from the date of its submission.

Amendment XXI

Passed by Congress February 20, 1933. Ratified December 5, 1933.

Section 1

The eighteenth article of amendment to the Constitution of the United States is hereby repealed.

Section 2

The transportation or importation into any State, Territory, or Possession of the United States for delivery or use therein of intoxicating liquors, in violation of the laws thereof, is hereby prohibited.

Section 3

This article shall be inoperative unless it shall have been ratified as an amendment to the Constitution by conventions in the several States, as provided in the Constitution, within seven years from the date of the submission hereof to the States by the Congress.

Amendment XXII

Passed by Congress March 21, 1947. Ratified February 27, 1951.

Section 1

No person shall be elected to the office of the President more than twice, and no person who has held the office of President, or acted as President, for more than two years of a term to which some other person was elected President shall be elected to the office of President more than once. But this Article shall not apply to any person holding the office of President when this Article was proposed by Congress, and shall not prevent any person who may be holding the office of President, or acting as President, during the term within which this Article becomes operative from holding the office of President or acting as President during the remainder of such term.

Section 2

This article shall be inoperative unless it shall have been ratified as an amendment to the Constitution by the legislatures of three fourths of the several States within seven years from the date of its submission to the States by the Congress.

Amendment XXIII

Passed by Congress June 16, 1960. Ratified March 29, 1961.

Section 1
The District constituting the seat of Government of the United States shall appoint in such manner as Congress may direct:

A number of electors of President and Vice President equal to the whole number of Senators and Representatives in Congress to which the District would be entitled if it were a State, but in no event more than the least populous State; they shall be in addition to those appointed by the States, but they shall be considered, for the purposes of the election of President and Vice President, to be electors appointed by a State; and they shall meet in the District and perform such duties as provided by the twelfth article of amendment.

Section 2
The Congress shall have power to enforce this article by appropriate legislation.

Amendment XXIV

Passed by Congress August 27, 1962. Ratified January 23, 1964.

Section 1
The right of citizens of the United States to vote in any primary or other election for President or Vice President, for electors for President or Vice President, or for Senator or Representative in Congress, shall not be denied or abridged by the United States or any State by reason of failure to pay poll tax or other tax.

Section 2
The Congress shall have power to enforce this article by appropriate legislation.

Amendment XXV

Passed by Congress July 6, 1965. Ratified February 10, 1967.
Note: Article II, section 1, of the Constitution was affected by the 25th amendment.

Section 1
In case of the removal of the President from office or of his death or resignation, the Vice President shall become President.

Section 2
Whenever there is a vacancy in the office of the Vice President, the President shall nominate a Vice President who shall take office upon confirmation by a majority vote of both Houses of Congress.

Section 3
Whenever the President transmits to the President pro tempore of the Senate and the Speaker of the House of Representatives his written declaration that he is unable to discharge the powers and duties of his office, and until he transmits to them a written declaration to the contrary, such powers and duties shall be discharged by the Vice President as Acting President.

Section 4
Whenever the Vice President and a majority of either the principal officers of the executive departments or of such other body as Congress may by law provide, transmit to the President pro tempore of the Senate and the Speaker of the House of Representatives their written declaration that the President is unable to discharge the powers and duties of his office, the Vice President shall immediately assume the powers and duties of the office as Acting President.

Thereafter, when the President transmits to the President pro tempore of the Senate and the Speaker of the House of Representatives his written declaration that no inability exists, he shall resume the powers and duties of his office unless the Vice President and a majority of either the principal officers of the executive department or of such other body as Congress may by law provide, transmit within four days to the President pro tempore of the Senate and the Speaker of the House of Representatives their written declaration that the President is unable to discharge the powers and duties of his office. Thereupon Congress shall decide the issue, assembling within forty-eight hours for that purpose if not in session. If the Congress, within twenty-one days after receipt of the latter written declaration, or, if Congress is not in session, within twenty-one days after Congress is required to assemble, determines by two-thirds vote of both Houses that the President is unable to discharge the powers and duties of his office, the Vice President shall continue to discharge the same as Acting President; otherwise, the President shall resume the powers and duties of his office.

Amendment XXVI

Passed by Congress March 23, 1971. Ratified July 1, 1971.

Note: Amendment 14, section 2, of the Constitution was modified by section 1 of the 26th amendment.

Section 1
The right of citizens of the United States, who are eighteen years of age or older, to vote shall not be denied or abridged by the United States or by any State on account of age.

Section 2
The Congress shall have power to enforce this article by appropriate legislation.

Amendment XXVII

Originally proposed <u>Sept. 25, 1789.</u> Ratified May 7, 1992.

No law, varying the compensation for the services of the Senators and Representatives, shall take effect, until an election of representatives shall have intervened.

NOTE 1: For a Millennium (1000 years) all nations will enjoy peace by being guided by the Original Intent of this God-inspired document. The uninspired Amendments 16 through 27 (except 18 which needs revision to cover all other harmful drugs) will probably be rescinded.

NOTE 2: Request families share copies of this document and by annual review gain a broad understanding, thus becoming "Constitutional Conservative". In unity Americans can bind "bloated government" down by chains of the Constitution and restore our God inspired Constitution Republic.

THE CHRONOLOGICAL O.T. DATED
TABLE OF CONTENTS

Table of Contents: Millennial Chronological Old Testament Of Jehovah

The Book Of II Kings:		
Chapters 1–14	About 874–730 B.C.	121
The Book Of II Chronicles:		
Chapters 10–28	About 924–730 B.C.	146
The Book Of Joel	About 800 B.C.	172
The Book Of Jonah	About 794 B.C.	177
The Book Of Hosea	About 787 B.C.	181
The Book Of Amos	About 784 B.C.	194
The Book Of Isaiah	About 734 B.C.	204
The Book Of II Chronicles:		
Chapters 29–35	About 726–537B.C.	279
The Book Of II Kings:		
Chapters 15–23	About 726–598 B.C.	293
The Book Of Micah	About 722 B.C.	311
The Book Of Jeremiah	About 634 B.C.	319
The Book Of Nahum	About 626–570 B.C.	401
The Book Of Zephaniah	About 624 B.C.	405
The Book Of Obadiah	About 614 B.C.	410
The Book Of Daniel	About 606 B.C.	414
The Book Of Habakkuk	About 604 B.C.	438
The Book Of Ezekiel	About 602 B.C.	443
The Book Of II Chronicles:		
Chapter 36 (Bk)	About 609–484 B.C.	519
The Book Of II Kings:		
Chapters 24 (Bk)	About 587–550 B.C.	522
The Book Of The Lamentations	About 584 B.C.	527
The Book Of Esther	About 524 B.C.	535
The Book Of Haggai	About 519 B.C.	548
The Book Of Zechariah	About 517 B.C.	552
The Book Of Ezra	About 458 B.C.	566
The Book Of Nehemiah	About 444 B.C.	582
The Book Of Malachi	About 424 B.C.	604

The approximate dates listed here can be verified in the KJV Bible. The apostle Paul, who was a student of the Great teacher Gamaliel at the time of Christ, left long unnoticed clues about the number of years between Abraham's sacrifice on Moriah and Moses receiving the 10 Commandments which was 430 years. Also in Acts (see Acts 13:20) he tells us that the period of Galatians (see Galatians 3:17) lasted 450 years. All other periods are easily tallied. With this information our approximate dating of the testaments is fairly accurate.

THE IMPORTANCE OF IMMANUEL VELIKOVSKY

Biblical references are listed by the author. The writings of Velikovsky are probably the best researched in the world. His books support his seven earned doctorates. His book, *Earth in Upheaval,* provides an understanding of cataclysms since the days of Adam which move the theories of this book into the realm of scientific probability. The reader should ask and answer this one simple question: should the Jew, Native American, or Christian of the twenty-first century permit that the works of one of the world's most well-educated men whose research has no peer be censored by the educational and publishing empires?

Immanuel was the son of one of the first Jews to return to the Holy Land after the Balfour Declaration. Immanuel received an education that appears to go beyond his peers. He received an independently earned PhD in seven separate disciplines and published (against great censorship odds) a book on each subject. He was a psychologist in Vienna with Freud and a recognized contemporary of Albert Einstein.

On the day of his death Einstein (per an article in *Reader's Digest)* had a Velikovsky book open on his desk and said to whose present, "We must give the work of Velikovsky more credence."

On the fly covers of his books you can see the struggles he had to keep from total censorship, which is currently the condition.

The positions he took as a result of his research are too costly to existing education and publication systems when they are accepted.

Unless his works can be suppressed nearly every education/publication disciple has to go back to square one and reconstruct itself. Tenured college professors will resist such an unsettling experience to their last breath. They don't relish giving up the comfortable story retelling salaries and prestige. Their world is firmly founded on the college campus. Gods, such as Darwin,

Freud, Dewey, Russell, Shaw and others. Darwin just resurrected the unproven evolutionary theories of the Greeks in 500 B.C. Those theories are more in question for the lack of evidence than before Darwin took his historic voyage.

On Friday, 26 April, 2002, the following Associated Press release of a study by the Grants of Princeton University gave Darwin a king-pin theory of Galapagos Island finches' inability to crossbreed a serious setback in favor of mutilation by hybridization, as follows:

> The Galapagos Island finches once studied by Charles Darwin respond quickly to changes in food supply by evolving new beaks and body sizes, according to researchers who studied the birds for almost 30 years.
>
> Starting in 1973, husband-and-wife researchers Peter and Rosemary Grant of Princeton University have followed the evolutionary changes in two types of birds, the ground finch and the cactus finch, on Daphne Major, one of the Galapagos Islands.
>
> In a study appearing today in the journal Science, the Grants report that climate and weather have a dramatic effect on the evolutionary path the finches follow.
>
> Ground finches mostly eat small seeds, and their beaks have adapted to that purpose. When the weather turned dry in 1977, most of the plants that produce small seeds on Daphne Major were killed, leaving little food for finches with modest-sized beaks. Most died off, but some ground finches with bigger, more powerful beaks survived, because they could feed on the tougher seed of a plant called caltrop.
>
> This led, within a few generations, to ground finches evolving with beaks that were 4 percent bigger than those of their ancestors.
>
> When the rains returned in 1983, and smaller seeds were in ample supply, ground finches with the

smallest beaks became the more efficient feeders. Again, the average beak size changed, shrinking by 2.5 percent, in succeeding generations of ground finches.

The rains that started in 1983 swamped the prickly plants favored by the cactus finches, and only those birds with slightly blunter beaks were able to feed on seeds of other plants. Most female cactus finches starved, and the males mated with some ground finches.

This process put genes from the ground finches into the gene pool of the cactus finches. The Grants said the beaks of the cactus finches became blunter, more like those of the ground finches.

WORKS OF VELIKOVSKY
(Dates listed are dates of publication)

Worlds in Collision (1950)

His first book, *Worlds in Collision*, first printing by Laurell in 1967 and twelfth printing by Dell in 1973.

The author did earth-encircling research of myths and legends related to observable signs in the heavens during the days of the Miracles of Moses. Stories from around the whole world convince the reader that all the tribes of the earth observed the same thing. Scholars scoffed at his assertion that our petroleum reserves were thrown from the rings of Venus as it passed close to the earth to orbit nearer the sun. The Venus probes have verified Velikovsky's position.

Ages in Chaos (1952)

The book discusses conditions between the Exodus and the founding of Rome. Herein one learns that the early Egyptologists and educators expanded ancient history by over 800 years. They listed the names of Egyptian dynasties but added the names given to those dynasties by neighboring cultures, thus listing the same dynasty more than once on more than one occasion. The end result was that the First Pharaoh of Egypt was tallied to have established his kingdom over 800 years before the flood.

Once these dynasty systems had hardened like concrete in the minds of scholars and Egyptologists there was no more questioning of the B.C. dating involved. The scholars then pointed to their erroneous dating as proof positive that Bible dating was in error and probably not a history but a myth.

Carnal man does not want to deal with a living God who will hold him accountable for his acts on a day of judgment. A large portion of today's "educated" population refuse to unsettle their consciences by Bible reading or conformity to the principles for joyous living taught within its pages.

In none of his books does Velikovsky appeal to the Bible as evidence, only to his research which invariably confirms the authenticity of the Bible without mentioning it.

Earth in Upheaval (1955)

Probably the best book for laymen to read is *Earth in Upheaval,* published by Doubleday and Company, Inc., in 1955.

Velikovsky's research to prepare this book deprives the evolutionists of the eons of stable times required to support their theories. The chapters on catastrophism and the evidence of cataclysms proven to take place in the 6,000 years of earth's history is an educational breakthrough.

Mutation within a species is a fact that confuses the issue. Nevertheless, since the 500 B.C. golden age of Greece no instance of the evolution of new species has been conclusively proved.

When the author was in high school the 50 to 60,000 years for the first Ice Age was taught as a proven fact. Velikovsky proved to the scientific community that carbon dating was not a perfect measuring stick.

But via carbon dating just within the lifetime of the author, the Ice Age has been reduced to between six and eight thousand years. My rule of thumb is to divide carbon dating systems by two to get nearer the truth.

This brings the Ice Age down. It probably developed as the natural result of evaporative cooling caused by the earth having been totally immersed in flood water for 150 days. I'm grateful to Velikovsky for bringing a measure of common sense to carbon dating.

Man and all animal species were much larger and healthier during the Adamic Dispensation prior to the flood. For proof, travel a couple of blocks west of La Brea Street on West Wilshire Blvd in Los Angeles and see those doubly large species with your own eyes. The museum claims they cannot understand why these large animals and dinosaurs became so suddenly and universally extinct.

Of course the last thing they would turn to as explanation would be the biblical account of the flood.

Christ said that hypocrites would look beyond the mark. These "scientists" are not willing to think of the time of extinction as being about 2473 B.C. They prefer extinction having taken place in billions of years to match the oft-repeated theory of evolution. Note that truth does not get nor have to be monotonously repeated for fear it will be questioned by some free spirit.

In summary, returning to *Earth in Upheaval,* it will probably be Velikovsky's best book because the extensive research has not and cannot be refuted.

Oedipus and Akhnaton (1960)

Oedipus and Akhnaton was published by Doubleday and Co., Inc., in 1960. In this book the author exposes the historical facts convoluted into myths by Freud to sell the public on the universality of the Oedipus complex which Freud was guilty of and wished to convince all other men on earth that they secretly desired mating with their mothers.

Sorry, but most men have never had that unholy temptation. Velikovsky challenges much of the basic framework of psychology as the hoped-for cure to social ills. The success rate and the impact of psychology upon our twenty-first century society is decidedly a negative. A few truths have been learned but acceptance of older false theories had had a destructive impact on society.

A careful reading of this book will help sort out the wheat from the refuse.

People of the Sea (1977)

In this book Velikovsky uses rather standard archaeological practices to restore pottery and trace its time and origin. Again the book becomes a testament that current Egyptologists have expanded time B.C. by over 800 years erroneously.

Ramses II and his Time (1978)

Velikovsky's exhaustive research in preparing this book establishes facts about the date of Ramses II that would be hard for any sensible person to refute. How can the Egyptologists like Cecil B. DeMille place Ramses II before 1400 B.C. when Velikovsky has unearthed both legs of a correspondence between Nebuchadnezzar and Ramses about their intellectually handicapped daughters. Ramses II fought Nebuchadnezzar's minions at KadeshCarchemish about 610 B.C. which is about 964 years after the Exodus. The reader is urged to read the evidence presented in these books.

Mankind in Amnesia (1982)

I have not been able as yet to acquire a copy of this book but plan to do so. One theme I understand it develops is that there are very few detailed records made during cataclysmic events such as the division of the earth in the days of Peleg in about 2300 B.C. Unfortunately, survival takes precedence over record keeping in most situations.

Stargazers and Gravediggers (1983)

This is Velikovsky's summary of the battles he had to fight to overcome and publish in the face of scholarly "scientists" who fought to keep his work suppressed.

It illustrates the greater need for truth seekers to obtain his works and read them. Hopefully, the demand could require Republication of the WORKS OF VELIKOVSKY.

Before the Day Breaks (whether published or not is unknown to the author)
The Test of Time (whether published or not is unknown to the author)

There are also two books written on the works of Velikovsky, the first by ten "scientific" opponents. They do not produce negative evidence but to the reader seem to be telling Velikovsky, "If you won't play by our well-defined monotonous rules we will take our ball and bat and go home."

The second group of ten scientists give instance after instance where new concepts developed by Velikovsky have been proven over the years by new tests and evidence.

The bottom line is any of these "censored" books can be obtained by inter-library loan.

Velikovsky's books are unique because they study the conditions parallel to the biblical account from 500 to 4000 B.C. They present a fresh breath of air to the early history of mankind. The implications of what he has revealed to the scholastic world are a farreaching fresh opportunity to structure factual ancient history independently of the stale concepts of psychology, Egyptology and evolution.

Note: because *Earth in Upheaval* and other of Velikovsky's works are so difficult to obtain due to "educational" censorship, please examine a new book by Jerome Horowitz, a lifelong successful attorney and author of books. His examination of evolution from a courts evidence position is excellent. The name of the book is *Evolution: Is it Science or Faith? By* Jerome Horowitz.

Second Edition by Walter C. Lichfield
and other family members.
Books listed under Lichfield Books, are also listed by
title, under Bible(s), Family and Parent coalition.

The Millennial Chronologically Dated Old Testament
of Jehovah,   Vol. I ISBN 1 594677 21 2

The Millennial Chronologically Dated Old Testament
of Jehovah,   Vol. II ISBN 1 594677 19 0

The Millennial Chronologically Dated New Testament
of Jesus the Christ   ISBN 1 594677 15 8

The Millennial Chronological Bible Info Book
                               ISBN 1 594677 17 4

Refining Our Best Resources: Our Children
                               ISBN 1 594677 26 3

Fanciful Bear Stories for Small Kids & Factual Bear
Stories for Big Kids   ISBN 1 594677 14 X

Creationist Theories Drawn from the Bible by Curtis
Hatfield (close friend of WCL)   ISBN 1 594676 31 3

Pocket full of Melodies and Poems * by
Wilma Browning Lichfield.

Order above listed books from
www.Xulonpress.com, also by 2005 they may be ordered
at www.barnesandnoble.com, www.wlamart.com,
www.borders.com and www.amazon.com.

* When completed will be available under Lichfield books.

Printed in the United States
25613LVS00005B/142

9 781594 676314